Voices of Tuscany

Publishing project
developed in collaboration with:

REGIONE TOSCANA
Culture, Tourism and Trade Council
www.regione.toscana.it

TOSCANA PROMOZIONE
Economic Promotion Agency of Tuscany
Villa Fabbricotti
Via Vittorio Emanuele II, 62-64
Florence
www.toscanapromozione.it

Publishing coordination by:
Iniziative Speciali, De Agostini Libri

Director
Andrea Pasquino

Texts: Giorgio De Martino

Iconography by Toscana Promozione
Photographic Archive, DeA Picture Library.
Photos by Giuseppe Moscato,
Luca Rossetti, MARIOevaMULAS.

*A special thanks to Giuseppe Moscato
for generously authorising the use
of photographs from his own archive.*

WS White Star Publishers® is a registered trademark
property of De Agostini Libri S.p.A.

© 2014 De Agostini Libri S.p.A.
Via G. da Verrazano, 15
28100 Novara, Italy

www.whitestar.it - www.deagostini.it

© 2014 Toscana Promozione

© 2014 Almud Edizioni Musicali s.r.l.
info@almudmusic.com

IBSN 978-88-544-0827-2

1 2 3 4 5 6   18 17 16 15 14

Printing: DEAPRINTING, Novara 2014

Voices of Tuscany

DISCOVER THE LAND OF GENIUS AND BEAUTY

Giorgio De Martino

WHITE STAR PUBLISHERS

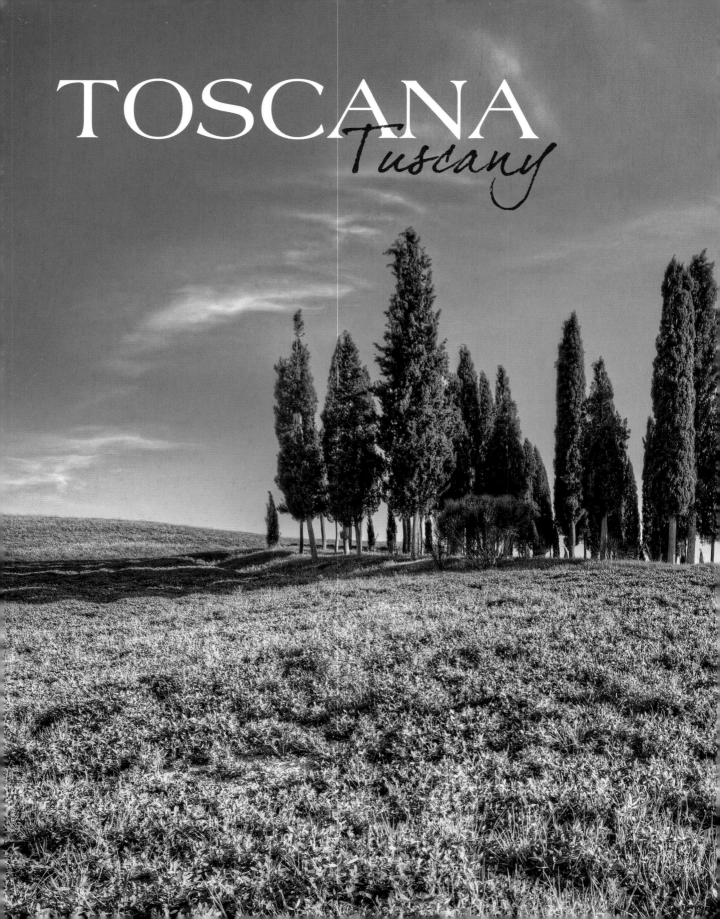

TOSCANA
Tuscany

My memories of Tuscany are stored
deep down in the depths of my soul.
They accompany me wherever I go,
because I am the product of this land,
the sum total of my past, my experiences
and my childhood dreams.

Andrea Bocelli

VOICES OF TUSCANY

Tuscany is a region of the soul.
It is impossible to regarded it as
a simple geographical location,
to be merely "visited". Tuscany
must be felt, lived, loved.
The paths to understanding and
falling madly in love with it are not
marked on maps or in guidebooks.
They crop up everywhere, in the
colours of the sunset, in the gaiety
of a steaming dish, in the shadow of
a rural church, in the playful combat
of a country fair, in the casual chats
with a local farmer met by chance
in a blazing field of sunflowers. And
again, in the warmth of a spa, in a
horse ride along one of the so-called
"strade bianche", in the skyline of a
medieval village, in a lavish platter
of cheese served with wine, in the
intense fragrances of a country lane,
in a barefoot walk along a beach,
in the ancient art of a museum,
or in a trinket handcrafted before
your very eyes.
Tuscany's inherent splendour is not
sufficient to reveal it in all its glory.
Its picture-postcard landscapes -
veritable paradises regained - are

only a piece of the puzzle of emotions experienced by travellers to this land.

There is no single Tuscany, but rather a multitude of Tuscanies - one for every new set of eyes. Its inherent call to beauty (in art, nature, cuisine and lifestyle) blends with one's personal sensitivity and personality, to become 'experience'. To unfold in all its essence, Tuscany needs to be experienced first hand, just as to resound, a melody needs an interpreter.

Every stretch of land is like a musical score, with its staves, its dynamics, its accelerandos and its rallentandos. Every landscape, every flavour, every work of art, whether natural or man-made, has its own melody, intensity and colour, ready to be interpreted and taken on as one's own.

Tuscany is a land intimately linked with song. Not just because it is the homeland of Andrea Bocelli, but also (and he would say "especially") because it is the birth place of talents such as Giacomo Puccini, Pietro Mascagni, Alfredo Catalani, Mario Del Monaco, Ettore Bastianini, Galliano Masini and Mario Filippeschi.

Song forms part of Tuscany's soul. So much so that for many centuries the region has constituted a point of reference, a legendary place of discovery and nostalgia, for musicians, poets, painters and dreamers everywhere.

The "Voices of Tuscany" are those of the great personalities and ambassadors of beauty, born in these superb latitudes. They form a chorus that is unparalleled across the globe. They sing of the experiences of those who have flourished under this civilization, each in their particular walk of life, throughout the course of history. But there is another kind of "voice", able to speak to the traveller. It is the voice of time and wisdom, waiting to reveal an entire civilization in the splendour of a street market, in a form of cheese, in a medieval tower, and in a golf course.

There is a Tuscany for every new set of eyes. This publication does not set out to offer its own, nor yet to give space to all the voices of Tuscany. Rivers of ink have been spent on the region and its off-spring, and yet a thousand pages, brimming with addresses on what to do, see or eat, would not be sufficient to describe the subtle sea scent of the wind, or the fragrance of summer, sensual and full of promise, or the air redolent of rain just before a cloud burst, or the dance of the cypress trees in the autumn. The same may be said for a sheet of music, in which there exists no sign capable of making the difference between a trivial or a sublime performance: that is the preserve of a true artist, who is capable of interpreting the piece to perfection. Tuscany, we have said, is a region of the soul. It is the adopted homeland of anyone who elevates it to such. The "Voices of Tuscany" which, with their evocative sensations, sustain this journey through images and words (which take a deliberately arbitrary form, ordered only by geographical province), lay the ground for a stage that awaits its artist; a solo voice here detected in the reader. The latter may pick up and ponder on the elements most appealing to him, using them as starting points for his or her very own first-hand experience of Tuscany.

An added value of this emotive guide is the presence, as one leafs through the pages, of a privileged "voice", that of a friend, a travelling companion, with whom the reader can engage in a virtual duet: namely, Andrea Bocelli, one of the greatest legends of the third millennium. He, like no other, can communicate emotions, and indeed his songs (which arouse the enthusiasm of audiences worldwide) are not merely about music: Bocelli interprets a culture, a way of being that is profoundly rooted in Tuscany. When he sings, he embodies his land, made of intense relationships, generosity, common sense, healthy food, beauty, and the art of 'doing' with love.

This book is published by White Star Publisher, now part of the De Agostini Group. De Agostini, which developed the project, is a prestigious brand founded over a century ago - it is no coincidence - by a family of explorers.. The project is endorsed by an ideal institutional partner, Regione Toscana, and has been developed in collaboration with *Toscana Promozione,* which has overseen the entire editorial project. The author and all the parties involved wish to thank Andrea Bocelli (along with his staff) for lending himself with kindness and generosity to this "declaration of love". His voice, deep and sincere like his land, testifies to the uniqueness of one of the most beautiful and exciting places in the world.

How can one describe Tuscany?
It is almost impossible. It would take
a lifetime.

Mario Tobino

CONTENTS

● CARRARA
● MASSA

● PISTOIA

● LUCCA   ● PRATO

● PISA   ● FLORENCE

● LIVORNO

AREZZO ●

● SIENA

● GROSSETO

TUSCAN ARCHIPELAGO

PISA

The Tower of Pisa.

WHY LAJATICO

Symbols become sound and transform into meaning. It is as true of the words you are reading as it is of the starting point of our journey. The best way to listen to the "Voices of Tuscany" is to start with silence. Less than fifty kilometres from Pisa, in the Val d'Era, nature has crafted a natural, hillside setting offering, on the one side the Etruscan skyline of Volterra, and on the other a glimpse of the Tyrrhenian Sea. Lajatico, Andrea Bocelli's home town, is the site of a theatre dedicated to silence, created in 2006 without a single inch of cement. Here, for 364 days a year, the star attractions are peace and nature, in a green-grey land marked by the smell of hay and covered in spring by clover and white primroses. Once a year – during an event that we would love to go on for ever – the theatre's terraces are fitted out with thousands of seats, while the stage, changed from one edition to the next, hosts some of the greatest artists in the world, invited to sing and play by Andrea Bocelli.

STARS

Dozens of leading stars, including Andrea's colleague Placido Domingo, the young

and already legendary pianist Lang Lang (who professed to be extremely elated by this poetic and ancestral arena), Sarah Brightman, and a treasured guest of the calibre of David Foster, have come to Val d'Era and experienced its atmosphere, celebrating the venue with their talent. The next day, and for the rest of the year, the spectacular open air amphitheatre transforms back into a natural landscape, in which the only sounds to be heard are the chirping of birds and the humming of tractors.

THE MUSIC OF SILENCE

Certain lands are rich in symbols, traced over the centuries by men and nature. Tuscany overflows with such symbols. A traveller with an innate sensitivity can transform them into sounds, into voices conveying emotions and values. We are all called upon to contribute to this process, recognising the symbols (in an experience involving sight, hearing, touch, smell and taste) and turning them into feelings, experience and memory. The most essential instrument is not a camera, but rather an openness to all that is new. At the start of a journey, silence can be a powerful instrument to prepare and make room for new input.

The theatre of silence, first edition.

The peace of this land is given by its rolling hills, cultivated fields, vineyards and olive trees, in a landscape dotted with small plots, confirming the fact that the local families have not abandoned their farms, but rather work hard to preserve their small properties. Andrea Bocelli, who, in addition to his theatre in Lajatico, also named his autobiography after silence (*The music of silence*), has learned to listen to the voice of these landscapes, picking up on their symbols and turning them into interior spaces, so as to act as emotional multipliers.

This he does by riding through the countryside, far from the madding crowds, amidst the Cabernet, Sangiovese and Merlot vineyards, breathing in the perfumes of the Lari cherries and Volterra truffles, enjoying the scent of the Mediterranean 'macchia', and savouring the bright green reflections of an oil so intense as to be a star attraction rather than a mere condiment. Here, in the heart of a peasant culture, born to a close-knit family – like many in Tuscany – and motivated by the ethics of passion, work and commitment, Andrea learned

a set of values that are the key to his success and that he transmits into his songs (singing, as he does, about what he knows and who he is).

WINE ROUTE
One of the two architects who designed the theatre of silence is Andrea's brother, who also carries on the family's passion for wine-making. Indeed, moving a few hundred meters downhill towards the village of La Sterza, his grandfather's refurbished cellars house small wooden barrels in which wine is left to age for two to three years. Here is an example of collaboration resulting in excellence that many families in Tuscany take as their model, likewise devoting their lives to caring for the earth and its products. The Wine Route is a scenic itinerary that winds through the hills of Val d'Era and the Lower Valdarno. In addition to Lajatico, it includes places such as Casciana Terme, whose lime-sulphur springs flow at a constant temperature of 36 °C, as well as Pieve di San Martino in Palaia, the Castle of Lari, Peccioli with its wine bars and workshops, and a mysterious church,

Left, coutryside around Volterra. Above, vineyards in Valdarno.

the "Madonna delle Serre", site of a series of miracles in the 17th century, and still today the final destination of numerous pilgrimages and torch lit processions.

VOLTERRA STONE AND ALABASTER
Known as the city of wind, Volterra overlooks the valleys of the rivers Cecina and Era. Once an important Etruscan centre, the city rises above a dried up sea (offering considerable salt deposits) and overlooks the so-called "Balze" cliffs, a mixture of sandy soil and clay that in ancient times often yielded, changing the geological structure and creating vertiginous precipices. Volterra's history is inextricably linked with the surreal, monochrome splendour of its stone. Impressive tower-houses and monuments (such as the 13th century Palazzo dei Priori, whose mullioned windows overlook the heart of Volterra, the Romanesque Cathedral and octagonal Baptistery, and the remains of the Roman theatre from the 1st century BC) contrast with the soft, translucent alabaster here masterfully worked.

WANDERING THROUGH VAL DI CECINA
Many hiking trails are found among the rolling hills of Pisa, with their multitude of cereal and grazing fields. Numerous trekking or mountain biking routes (sometimes practicable by car) ensure continuous surprises. One can venture along the northern valleys, amidst mills, chestnut groves, ancient shrines, Etruscan city walls and breathtaking views of the cliffs, through the Upper Val d'Era, amidst churches, villas and farms, and through the Monte Nero, with its

gorges and precipices, or again explore the area's clay basins, in a landscape marked by small, time-worn churches.

MUCCO PISANO BEEF
The baths at San Giuliano Terme were already popular at the time of the Etruscans and Romans. As from the 1700s, much of the nobility of Europe took up residence here. Frequent guests included George IV of England, Mary Shelley, Gustav of Sweden, Ibrahim Pasha of Egypt and the Italian playwright Carlo Goldoni. Close to the art cities of Pisa and Lucca, but also to the Apennines, a spectacular coastline comprising the natural Parco Marittimo of San Rossore, the social life of Versilia, and the sports scene of the international golf centre of Tirrenia, San Giuliano is one of the few places where one can still eat "Mucco Pisano" beef. In the 1980s, this large, dark cow, first cross-breed three centuries ago, was in danger of extinction. Today it is considered a valued breed, closely monitored due to its exceptional quality characteristics. In addition to stews and braised meats, food lovers can enjoy the 'mucco bresaola', a cold meat produced by massaging the beef for a prolonged period of time and allowing it to rest for weeks in a vat of herbs, including bitter oranges, lemon, juniper berries and thyme.

SAN MINIATO
The scent of history, leather and white truffle. Arising on the top of three hills, San Miniato overlooks the River Arno and is situated midway between Pisa and Florence (whose influence can be felt in terms of the local dialect). An aristocratic

Roofs of Volterra.

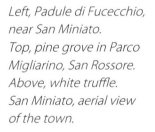

Left, Padule di Fucecchio, near San Miniato.
Top, pine grove in Parco Migliarino, San Rossore.
Above, white truffle.
San Miniato, aerial view of the town.

'Palio del Cuoio' (literally, the leather race), inaugurated some thirty years ago, and its 'Corsa dei Caratelli' (a race in small barrels that historically contained the tannin used in tanning hides).
Situated along the Via Francigena and surrounded by tilled fields and woods rich in precious tubers, San Miniato proudly remembers the 5.5-pound truffle found in 1954 and donated to the American President Eisenhower.

VESPA!

The 1953 film "Roman Holiday", a back-to-front Cinderella story starring Gregory Peck and Audrey Hepburn, earned the Vespa world-acclaimed fame. Piaggio's renowned two-wheeler came to life in Pontedera, home to the company's historic headquarters and, since 2000, to the Piaggio Museum: three thousand square metres housing a century of excellence in scooter creativity and technology, as testified by unique pieces that have made the history of Italian and worldwide transport, including the Vespa decorated by Salvador Dali and the fully faired models produced in the 1950s to compete in speed and endurance competitions. Not surprisingly, the cover of *Incanto,* one of Bocelli's most popular albums, sees Andrea standing next to a Vespa.

THE LEANING TOWER

Striking, exotic, mysterious, studenty, poetic and bold, the city of Pisa, crossed by the River Arno, boasts the stunning Campo dei Miracoli, the UNESCO World Heritage Site comprising the world-famed leaning tower. While (fortunately) not a

centre of power built by the Lombards in the 8th century, between 1217 and 1223 Frederick II chose the site for his fortress and the fortified seat of the Imperial Vicar of Tuscany. Centuries later, the young Napoleon Bonaparte visited San Miniato on several occasions. Promoted to Diocese in 1622, it was soon endowed with an Episcopal Seminary for new generations of monks. The Cathedral includes a tower named after "Matilda", in tribute to a local legend whereby Matilda of Canossa, a powerful feudatory of the Middle Ages, was born here at the time of the Holy Roman Empire.

PALIO DEL CUOIO

San Miniato has never forsaken its traditions, and indeed sometimes reinvents them. One example is the

Piazza dei Miracoli, Pisa.

funfair, the square has often seen curious travellers enjoy a spot of fun as they take a photograph trying to hold up the Leaning Tower. Thanks to its inhabitants and to its Universities, Pisa is a lively, unaffected city that has never lost its sense of identity. The renowned bell tower, set in the spectacular Piazza del Duomo and built between the twelfth and 14th century, began to tilt during construction, due to inadequate foundations.

It is considered one of the seven wonders of the modern world, alongside the Great Wall of China and the Taj Mahal in India. A triumph of curvature, it measures fifty-six metres in height, weighs fifteen tons and has a tilt of over two and a half metres. Scientists and amateurs around the globe passionately monitor its silent movement and the technological countermeasures taken for its protection, especially via the web.

BEYOND THE TOWER

While the Campo dei Miracoli is a pleasant place to linger, one must not forget that, beyond this magic rectangle - a melting pot of (often greedy) amateur shots - lies Pisa, a city just waiting to be discovered. Situated eight kilometres from the sea, and standing on the immense green lawn of the ancient Maritime Republic, like an architectural dream come true, lie the Baptistery, with its Romanesque and Gothic influences, and the Cathedral, with its wealth of paintings, including some by Andrea del Sarto and Domenico Beccafumi, and its sculptural wonders, such as the 14-century marble pulpit by Giovanni Pisano.

HOLY EARTH IN PISA

The monumental cemetery situated near the Cathedral is said to contain soil brought back from Palestine by the Crusaders in the 1200s. The painted walls, damaged by World War II, are an amazing testimony of medieval art. The 14th century fresco by Buonamico Buffalmacco, depicting the *Triumph of Death,* inspired Franz Liszt to compose his *Totentanz,* a paraphrase on the Gregorian chant *Dies Irae.*

GALILEO GALILEI

Vincenzo Galilei was one of the greatest musicians of the late Renaissance, and a member of the group of artists and intellectuals, led by Count Bardi, to which we owe the birth of opera. His son, Galileo, a physicist, philosopher, astronomer and mathematician - in a word, the"father of modern science" - was born in Pisa in 1564. The "Domus Galileiana" - or home of Galileo, not to be confused with his birthplace (Casa Ammannati) in Via Giusti - is found in the 18th century "Palazzo della Specola", in Via Santa Maria, and collects memorabilia from the scientist's life, including a vast scientific library. The international airport of Pisa, named after Galileo Galilei, is an essential hub for the entire region.
Its continual expansion testifies to its record-breaking passenger traffic, which increases steadily by double digits. Given its strategic location (one kilometre from the centre of Pisa and just eighty kilometres from Florence) and the width of its runways, it has become the main airport of Tuscany.

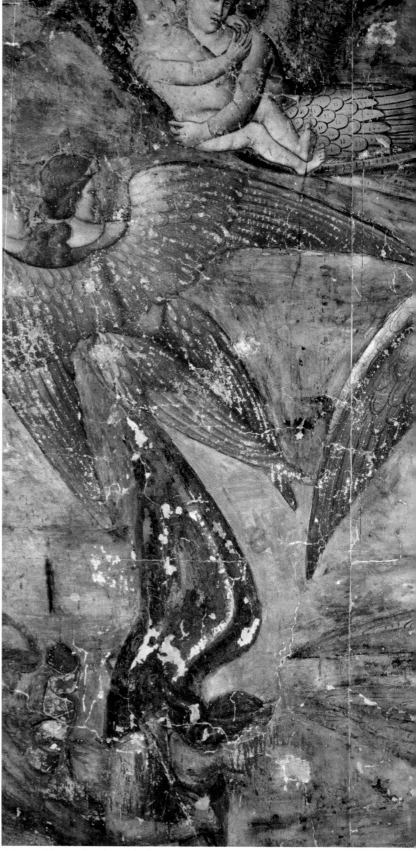

Above, Triumph of Death, fresco by Buffalmacco.

COLTANO RADIO CENTRE

A small town situated between Pisa
and Collesalvetti is home to a Medici
villa and to a further small building
- semi-abandoned for decades and
now in the process of being upgraded
- which represents the most important
monument to radio, a crucial venue for
the world history of communication.
Coltano is where the inventor of radio, the
Nobel Prize winner Guglielmo Marconi,
realised his first broadcasts to the world.
The centre was inaugurated officially in
1911 by King Vittorio Emanuele II, with a
special radio connection to Nova Scotia.
In 1931, a radio signal was transmitted
from Coltano that turned on the lights
of Christ Redeemer in Rio de Janeiro, in
a test of strength that emphasised the
importance of intercontinental radio
communications.

Right, Guglielmo Marconi with one of his first telegraphs.

*My Tuscany is not just hills,
olive groves and vineyards;
my Tuscany is also the sea:
I harbour a deep love for the mystery
of this immense mass, for this vast
space without borders, where the
imagination can run free.*

Andrea Bocelli

THE IDEAL CITY

The province of Livorno, situated across
a string of hills and plains washed by the
Tyrrhenian Sea, like a tightrope covering
the arc of the Tuscan Archipelago, is
superintended by its capital. Livorno, like
most of its surrounding towns, was built
on ancient settlements dating back
to Neolithic times.

The 'new' city was founded in the late
16th century when the Medici family,
who ruled Florence for over three
centuries, decided to develop the area
and to commission the 'ideal city' from
the architect Buontalenti. And so Livorno,
a fortified centre designed with an
orthogonal street system, is an example of
a city that predates its people.

The town conceals yet another side
of Tuscany, due to its patchwork of
ethnicities and successful contaminations.
Greeks, Jews, Englishmen, Dutchmen,
Armenians, Turks and Moors all enjoyed
the freedom of worship and hospitality
guaranteed by the city.

Heterogeneous communities have
integrated in the port town, enriching
it with their customs, dialects, flavours,
churches and cemeteries. To this day,
it is possible to pray in Livorno's

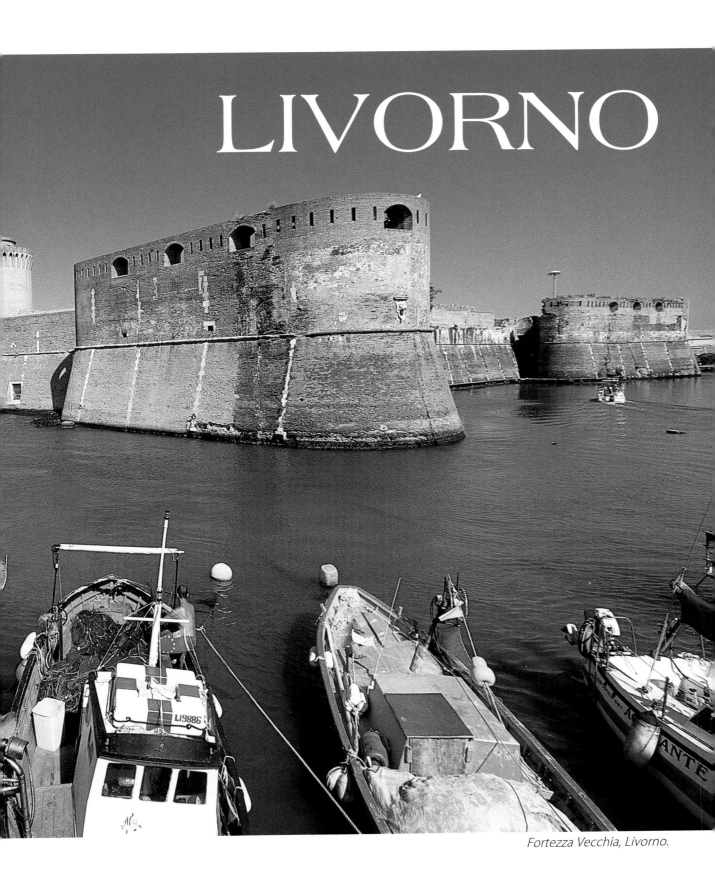

LIVORNO

Fortezza Vecchia, Livorno.

Armenian temple, Calvinist chapel, Jewish synagogue and Greek church. The result, is a close-knit, sanguine, engaging "Livornese identity" that is difficult to describe.

FORTEZZA VECCHIA, VENEZIA NUOVA

The city's most striking symbol is given by the bronze statues of the Four Moors that surround the monument to the Grand Duke Ferdinando I (in Piazza Micheli). The main statue, by Giovanni Bandini, was transported from Carrara by sea in 1601.
The Moors were added a quarter of a century later, by Pietro Tacca. Livorno is inclined to expand its attractions into imposing architectural structures, and indeed sometimes into entire neighbourhoods. The ancient Fortezza Vecchia, dominating the Porto Mediceo, comprises three ramparts and the 11th century tower known as the "Tower of Matilda"; the newer Fortezza Nuova was constructed by Buontalenti and is surrounded by a spectacular moat. The Venezia Nuova district, conceived at the start of the 1600s to face a boost in the city's demographics, develops behind the port in a maze of canals and houses whose foundations have been laid directly in the water, adopting a construction technique imported from the Venetian lagoon.

Above, view of Livorno.
Left, Terrazza Mascagni,
detail and I Quattro Mori.

STRONG FLAVOURS

The cuisine of Livorno, with its strong flavours, has been good-naturedly defined as 'quarrelsome' and 'populistic'. Resulting from a series of complex and exotic influences, the local culinary tradition often pivots on fish, as well as a considerable use of tomatoes (introduced by the Sephardic Jews). The most famous dish is the 'cacciucco', a fish soup, perhaps of Phonetician origin, that does justice to less noble fish, and that in the 16th century was used to feed the rowers chained to the galleys. Livorno, however, is not just about fish soup. There is fish aplenty, from cod to mullet, and from anchovies to sardines, but there are also "earth" dishes, such as chicken in aspic, stuffed artichokes and a soup known as "Bordatino alla Livornese", and desserts, including the 'castagnaccio', a chestnut cake traditionally prepared for the festivities of St. Catherine and St. Nicholas. The most typical local alcoholic beverage has Anglo-Saxon origins: it is the "ponce", a variant of punch, made with hot coffee, rum, sugar, lemon, and numerous other ingredients (including cayenne pepper).

GIOVANNI FATTORI

No artist has depicted the landscape of the Maremma area of Tuscany - that extraordinary microcosm that extends between Livorno and Grosseto, made up of beaches, cultivated hills, woods and traces of Etruscan civilization - more effectively than Giovanni Fattori (1825-1908). Born in Livorno, Fattori is the greatest exponent of the Macchiaioli artistic movement. In his works, the artist depicts Maremma, a land of brigands, peasants and 'butteri' (typical herdsmen

Left, venetian-style canal in Livorno.
Top, boat in a canal, Livorno.
Right, escalopes Livorno style and Caciucco.

Piazza Mascagni, Livorno.

on horseback), with poetic realism. In Via San Jacopo in Acquaviva, near Villa Mimbelli, the Museo Civico Giovanni Fattori offers three floors filled with his paintings, as well as works of other exponents of the macchiaioli and post-macchiaioli movements.

THE HOAX OF THE FALSE MODIGLIANIS

Livorno is also the home town of Amedeo Modigliani, a brilliant painter and sculptor from the early 1900s, famous for his stylised portraits of women. Legend has it that the artist, disheartened by the lack of understanding for his art, threw a number of statues into the Fosso Reale (or royal moat). In 1984, on the occasion of an exhibition on "Modì", as he is affectionately known, a search was led, which brought to the discovery of three heads, instantly celebrated by the most renowned critics as genuine. Days later it was discovered that the statues were blatantly fake and were actually produced by students as a gag - a hoax worthy of the rebelliously shrewd people of Livorno.

MASCAGNI AND MASINI

The opera *Cavalleria Rusticana* (1890), a story of love and blood adapted from a play by the same name written by Giovanni Verga, marked the breakthrough of realism in opera, and introduced a veritable revolution in the method of storytelling and singing. The tragedy is set in an archaic, late 19th century Sicily, although its composer, Pietro Mascagni (1863-1945), was actually born in Livorno. In addition to the Museo Mascagnano, which displays memorabilia, photographs and an extensive archive of letters, Livorno has named its Terrazza Mascagni after the romantic musician. The Terrazza, which provides pleasant walks along the seafront, is a place of metaphysical beauty, with its black and white chequerboard flooring and an infinite sequence of columns overlooking the island of Gorgona. An unforgettable interpreter of Mascagni's works is the tenor Galliano Masini (Livorno, 1896-Livorno, 1986), who, during his lifetime, brought his city to worldwide fame. A room of the 19th century Teatro Goldoni has been named after Masini, a man loved for his simplicity, directness and shrewdness, in the manner of his fellow citizens.

Above, tree-lined avenue.
Right, aerial view of Castagneto Carducci.

BATHING IN CULTURE

In Castiglioncello, one can rest on the beach in the shade of the pine trees, amidst sand and rock, between the sea and the Mediterranean 'macchia'. Considered an emblem of the Etruscan coast, the light found on this small promontory inspired the "Italian Impressionists", the followers of the Macchiaioli movement who gave life to the "School of Castiglioncello" on the estate of the patron Diego Martelli. Ever a holiday and culture destination, in 1962 Castiglioncello was the site of the filming of *Il Sorpasso*, starring Vittorio Gassman and Jean-Louis Trintignant, at a time when the town was enjoying its personal "Dolce Vita", regularly frequented by actors such as Marcello Mastroianni and Alberto Sordi. To this day, Castiglioncello enjoys a lively cultural scene, due to its festival of theatre and dance and a literary award, the ceremony of which takes place at the Castello Pasquini, an imposing structure built in the late 19th century as a mock medieval fortress.

POETRY LANE

The two rows of cypress trees that from the SS1 state road (Via Aurelia) rise as far as Bolgheri enjoy a literary as well as a landscape claim to fame, insofar as they were extolled in a famous poem by Giosué Carducci. Indeed, the small medieval village belongs to a municipality named after the poet, Castagneto Carducci. The straight road first leads to the Cappella di San Guido, and then up to the imposing, reddish Castello di Bolgheri, with its rectangular crenellated tower (an old fortalice now converted into a farm producing quality oil and wine).

POPULONIA, THE ETRUSCANS AND IRON

Populonia, overlooking the Gulf of Baratti (known for its silver sand beach), is the only Etruscan settlement found on the coast. A key mining and metallurgical centre in ancient times, it is still possible to see the remains of Etruscan walls and Roman buildings, as well as a necropolis

Above, the Populonia's fortress. Top right, Torre dell'Orologio and Palazzo Pretorio, Campiglia Marittima.

with mound, chamber and aedicule tombs (dating from the 8th to the 2nd century BC). Populonia re-flourished in the Middle Ages, during which time a fortress was built, dominating the Acropolis to this day. In the village, one can visit the Museo Gasparri, a private collection of artefacts, sarcophagi and funerary statues. Populonia lies in the municipality of Piombino, the main port connecting mainland Italy to the island of Elba and an industrial city with an interesting historic centre. Piombino also boasts a nearby coast of great beauty - the Sterpaia coastal park - featuring a mixture of sand dunes and age-old oak trees.

WHITE ROADS

Tuscany and horses have always been a winning combination. Horses for sport purposes, but also as a spectacular means of transport, and as a symbol of a renewed attention to nature and its rhythms, enabling travellers to roam through the region's countryside, forests and villages.

One can explore a goodly part of the province of Livorno on horseback. One of the routes most dear to Andrea Bocelli, a skilled horseman, is the one linking Lajatico to the sea at Cecina, proceeding towards Campiglia Marittima along trails that meander through vineyards and olive groves, continuing as far as Montieri and the Colline Metallifere (or metal-bearing hills), and then completing the circle by heading back towards Casole d'Elsa (near Siena). "An unforgettable experience," says Andrea. "Three hundred kilometres of adventure through woods, fields, and pure, uncontaminated nature."

METALS AND MYSTERIES

In the medieval village of Campiglia Marittima, which owes its fortunes to the local iron, copper, zinc and tin mines, stands a Romanesque church devoted to San Giovanni. Under the roof, on the façade, it is possible to admire an example of a "Sator Square," a Latin palindrome featuring five words (*sator, arepo, tenet, opera, rotas)*: the phrase can be read from right to left and vice versa. The inscription, related to Christian symbolism and hiding a somewhat dark side, may be found in other medieval places of worship, from England to Spain. Just three kilometres away, a hill top serves as the site of a fortified village, Rocca San Silvestro, which dominates an area devoted, since the time of the Etruscans, to the conversion of copper and silver lead. Its walls, which have withstood over a thousand years of history, bear witness to the interest of the Gherardesca counts in the area's mineral resources. The Rocca is now the heart of the Parco Minerario e Archeologico (Mineral and Acheological Park), offering a multitude of routes through old open-air mines.

BOCELLI, MALAPARTE AND THE PEOPLE OF TUSCANY

Curzio Malaparte, an author from Tuscany particularly dear to Bocelli, wrote scintillating passages on Livorno (with its "smells reminiscent of galleys and rocks"). Andrea frequently recommends a celebrated text from 1956, *Maledetti Toscani,* a poetic and witty declaration of love addressed to Tuscany and its people. These, according

People would speak to me about it [Livorno] as of a place of delight, as a theatre in which wonderful scenes unfold, and extraordinary meetings take place; a place where the most varied and unusual people come together, as if at home, and where one can collect the most valuable goods yielded by the earth and the sea. Pirates, merchants, sailors, their face burnt by the salt; blacks, Arabs, British and Greeks; coffee beans; Russians, hairy and melancholy; women from all climates, odalisques covered with veils, and Indians with a red bindi in the middle of their forehead; barrels of fragrant wine; piles of fabrics, drugs and blond tobacco; and ships, ship, ships, that come and go, filling the sky with clouds of smoke and flashes of white sails. They would speak of their city, describing its beauty and its graces with modest jealousy.

Curzio Malaparte

*Top left, landscape with sheaves.
Bottom left, horse harnesses.*

to Malaparte, believe they can give lessons to all and sundry, "because it was they who invented the Italian language". And indeed, none better than they can make fun of the most tragic situations, or create embarrassment during moments of elation. And yet, says the author, "it would be better if in Italy there were more Tuscans and fewer Italians, because, in their way of thinking, anyone who is not a free man is a stupid man."

ARCIPELAGO TOSCANO
Tuscan Archipelago

Island of Elba, Capo d'Enfola.

APHRODITE'S PEARLS

The largest marine park in Europe has
seven main islands: Elba, Giglio, Capraia,
Montecristo, Pianosa, Gorgona and Giannutri.
Legend has it that these are the pearls
of a necklace worn by Aphrodite, and
which the goddess inadvertently let fall
into the Tyrrhenian Sea, giving rise to the
archipelago. The islands are a triumph of
natural environments and tourist attractions.
Although just a few kilometres from the
mainland, they are a world apart, in terms of
flora, fauna and morphology: Gorgona, small
and wild; Montecristo, once the home of
monks, and later a source of inspiration for the
famous novel by Alexandre Dumas; Giannutri,
an important bird sanctuary, and a crucial
resting place for rare migrating species.

GIGLIO PORT AND CASTLE

Measuring twenty square kilometres of steep
granite cliffs and sandy beaches, Giglio boasts
the ruins of several century-old settlements.
Today, its towns cover just 10% of the
territory. The port reveals a Roman imprint,
while also featuring defensive towers linked

> *The island is healthy, the people good and the country very pleasant. (...)*
> *I'm here in a monastery at 600 meters above sea level, with a view of the Mediterranean, in the midst of a chestnut grove. (...) It is a very pleasant stay.*
> *Napoleon Bonaparte*

to the ferocious Saracen raids suffered by the island. The castle of Giglio, built by the people of Pisa in the 12th century, is an inhabited fortified complex on the summit of the island, made up of walls, rectangular and circular towers, and the imposing early medieval Rocca Aldobrandesca.

ELBA, WITH FLIPPERS AND PICKAXE

From the legendary waters of the coast, it is possible to climb to an altitude of one thousand meters, through the Mediterranean 'macchia' and across a chain of vineyards (where the rare dessert wine Aleatico is produced), to the top of Monte Capanne – reachable by cable car – offering a view of Corsica and the entire coast of Tuscany. At Elba, the bowels of the earth are a paradise of metals and minerals. The ancient Romans used the iron yielded by the fish-shaped island to produce the tips of their spears. As for the sea, the island's consortium of diving centres has opened schools for children and senior citizens, where students are taught to respect the local "tropical" sea, boasting groupers, barracudas, snappers and moray eels. Worthy of note, among the various ideal diving sites, are Capo Stella, Scoglietto in Portoferraio, Picchi di Pablo and Scoglio dell'Ogliera, where it is possible to visit the "wreck of Pomonte".

Above, Island of Elba: Portoferraio.
Right, Terranera Lake in Porto Azzurro.

The island offers plenty of opportunities for breath-held diving, snorkelling, kayaking, sailing and dolphin watching. There is even an underwater museum at Punta Polveraia, where a series of mythological sentries in white marble, ranging from Neptune to the Sleeping Venus, oversee a sunken garden: a sensory experience designed with the visually impaired in mind.

NAPOLEON

Napoleon Bonaparte, one of the greatest leaders of all times, was for ten months the (beloved) ruler of the island. His golden exile, between 1814 and 1815, is witnessed by two museums, in the buildings he chose as his residence: Villa dei Mulini in Portoferraio and the magnificent Villa San Martino, immersed in luxuriant green. The Foresiana library (set up care of the De Laugier cultural centre in Portoferraio) retains many of the two thousand valuable books donated to the city by the emperor.

ON MULE BACK

Up to fifty years ago, the mule was the most common means of travel, on an island criss-crossed by a network of paths and trails: essential routes connecting the coast to the villages established on high ground as a countermeasure against piracy.
Today, trips on mule back are once again popular, offering tourists an alternative approach to the island, scanned by an ancient rhythm.

GROSSETO

Maremma Horses.

SOUTHERN TUSCANY

The province of Grosseto - a land of earth and water, not always regimented by a coastline - models its works of art on itself, without the need for mediation or the mark of man. The splendour of this further Tuscany is made up of forests, natural parks, sandy shores, islands, dunes, lagoons, sulphur springs, mountains and pine groves reaching as far as the shore. It is made up of an amazing fauna, and a changing nature often fondly described as "rough". Not surprisingly, the main resource of this Etruscan region - the leading rural district of Europe - is tourism, which in summer multiplies the local population ten-fold. Here, tourism takes on a variety of forms: seaside tourism, backed by many a celebrated endorser (exponents of the worlds of literature, industry and politics); cultural tourism, supported by numerous archaeological sites and medieval and Renaissance villages; rural tourism, with a wealth of farm holidays and natural parks; spa tourism, with a multitude of shrines to wellbeing; and mountain and skiing tourism, in Mount Amiata (a volcanic massif bordering with the province of Siena, from the top of which visitors can enjoy the most

*Above, early sheaves
in Maremma.
Right, Grosseto, detail
of the Cathedral; rural
landscape; a view of the
medieval centre of Sorano.*

extensive and breathtaking scenery of central Italy). There is one last form of tourism, linked with food and wine, enabling visitors to explore the delights of Maremma beef, fish dishes and soups, prepared using excellent local farm products. And all this, served with a glass of Morellino di Scansano, of any one of the many noble wines produced in the province.

GOLDEN WINDS

The sails that dot the Grosseto coastline offer the surreal and rebellious spectacle of a flourish of flowers in a sea-blue meadow. The Federazione Italiana Vela (Italian Sailing Federation) counts just shy of twenty affiliated educational and sports centres, in a province whose generous warm winds make the coast between Follonica and the Argentario promontory a paradise for regattas and other sailing events, for champions and beginners alike. Surrounded by the sea on three sides, punctuated by ancient fortifications offering protection against pirates, and embellished by a pine grove, Punta Ala, a seaside resort south of Follonica, is the brith place of "Luna Rossa", the famous sailing boat renowned for its successes in the

Above: Porto Santo Stefano, Monte Argentario. Top: Follonica beach.

Above, Province's builiding in Dante Square, Grosseto. Right, Cathedral.

America's Cup. This is the ideal place in which to practice all water sports, from surfing to sailing and water skiing. Its sea bed, between the mainland coast and the island known as "dello Sparviero" (named after a medieval watch tower) is a popular destination with scuba diving enthusiasts. Visitors who tire of the sea simply need turn their back to the Tyrrhenian Sea and enjoy the generous gifts offered by the vast Mediterranean 'macchia', with a spot of golf, polo or horse riding.

GROSSETO

A city with an ancient heart, enclosed in a hexagonal rampart. The history of Grosseto is filled with rises and falls. A 16th century reclamation, at the hands of the Medici family, caused the revival of the town's 13th century glory, when Frederick II, Duke of Swabia, used to frequent Grosseto, with poets and nobles in his train. However, the threat of water logging, and consequently of malaria, soon returned to plaque the city, which had to wait for the Congress of Vienna, when Ferdinand III of Tuscany took up the reclamation works, before enjoying a further revival. Among the many attractions of the Old Town stands out the Cathedral (late 13th century), designed by Sozzo di Rustichino and renovated several times throughout the ages. The 19th century façade echoes the Romanesque style, and is covered with two-tone strips of red and white marble. Worthy of note on the inside is a 15th century crucifix and an imposing baptismal font by Antonio Ghini.

MAREMMA NATURAL PARK

Between mountains, pine groves, marshes and miles of uncontaminated beaches, without the trace of a sun umbrella or car park, lies the Parco Naturale della Maremma, ranging for a vast ten thousand hectares. This wild and changing environment stretches from the Palude della Trappola to the Monti dell'Uccellina, covering the coastline that from Principina a Mare reaches as far as Talamone. There are a multitude of trails to wander along, preferably in the company of a guide, and many

protected species to be seen. The mouth of the River Ombrone provides shelter to colonies of marsh birds, as well as cows, wild horses, wild boar, deer and foxes. On looking upwards, it is possible to admire peregrine falcons, wild ducks and jays. Moreover, it is not uncommon, in November, to come upon the two meter wingspan of a crane, on route from the swampy Scandinavian woods to the warmth of North Africa.

Above: an old Spanish mill, Orbetello lagoon. Top right, a Maremma 'buttero'.

HOME-GROWN COWBOYS

Maremma is a land of butteri, typical farmers on horseback, dressed in leather and corduroy, who follow stallions and cows through abandoned agricultural areas and grasslands used for grazing semi-wild livestock. The Italian answer to the American cowboy and the Argentine gaucho, the buttero performs the solitary work of watching over herds and taming horses. Indeed, in terms of taming horses, once the butteri got the better of none other than Buffalo Bill. The hero of the Wild West came to the area in the early 1900s to perform his Wild West Show, and was challenged by the Duke of Sermoneta, owner of several herds. Buffalo Bill accepted, unaware of the outstanding native stock of horses and riders, and indeed succumbed to the tenacity and resistance of the Maremma breeders.

LITTLE VENICE

Originally an island, inhabited as from ancient times, the Argentario gradually became a promontory due to the slow and remote accumulation of sand, which gave birth to the two strips of land that connect it to the mainland and to the isthmus on which Orbetello stands. The latter, known as the "Venice of Tuscany", is a jewel set almost

Vie Cave.

entirely in the lagoon by the same name, retaining Etruscan defensive walls and Spanish fortifications. It also boasts a WWF oasis that serves as a critical wintering site for more than two hundred species of waterfowl. Here, in recent decades, the "Black-winged Stilt", a graceful marsh wader, has returned to nest.

VIE CAVE

A number of deep, multimillenial trenches, known as "Vie Cave", "Cavoni" or "Tagliate", connect the three Etruscan sites of Sovana, Sorano and Pitigliano. The paths, carved in tufa and topped by walls reaching a height of one hundred feet, contain many traces of the toils endured by the people involved in its construction. The Vie Cave were used as strategic passageways against enemies, as well as short cuts and channels for directing rainwater. Set in the Parco Archeologico Città del Tufo, they connect several Etruscan necropoles, with monumental tombs scattered radially and produced in the soft local stone. In the Christian era, the evocative darkness that envelops these wounds in the rock has fostered the creation of niches that now guard reassuring holy images. For the same characteristics, the Vie Cave were once also a popular site for pagan rituals and night time processions. A walk along these paths, among moss, lichens, ivy and creepers, is a real must. Also worth a visit is the archaeological site of Sovana, whose most famous and scenic tomb is the so called "Tomba Ildebranda", entirely carved in rock. This Etruscan temple boasts six columns, capitals and traces of coloured stucco.

THE ECLECTIC GARDEN OF SPOERRI

The Garden deigned by Daniel Spoerri is a green mantle of contemporary art, a park-museum of wonder and shape, spanning sixteen hectares of nature and sculpture. Situated at Seggiano, on a large site located between the River Orcia and Monte Amiata, the Garden has acquired, since the early '90s, some one hundred sculptures, which integrate into the environment with ease, in a *work in progress* that expands year after year with new acquisitions. The Latin inscription *hic terminus haeret*, or "here is the end of all things", welcomes visitors to this magical space - now a Foundation - where the Swiss artist has gathered a rich collection of his own bronze compositions and of the works and installations of forty other artists, in part exponents of the "Nouveaux Realistes" and "Fluxus" movements. Alongside the route through the "Garden" (the official geographical name of this area on the slopes of Monte Amiata) and the vertical race of creativity between olive trees and sculptural forms, Spoerri chose to associate a natural itinerary featuring over forty species of plants identified by multilingual signs. Also in the province of Grosseto, in Garavicchio (near Capalbio), another art park, this time conceived by the French-American artist Niki de Saint Phalle, hosts a series of statues inspired by the Major Arcana of the Tarot cards.

SCENTED, HEALING WATERS

"Sometimes the gases rise from the canals to form a frayed blanket of fog that wafts across the road and invades the fields in a sea of cream, creating a cloud-like scene. Out of the white, rises a fruit tree, a fence, half a sheep. It is almost as if someone had passed by with one of those machines that create fake fog on film sets. But if anyone was in any doubt, the scent would be enough to dispel any misgivings." This is how the writer Niccolò Ammaniti describes the thermal baths of Saturnia, a hamlet near Manciano. Saturnia, with its "Porta Romana" on the ancient Via Clodia (3rd century BC), unsurprisingly known as the "road of the thermal baths", is famous for its hot sulphur springs (37 °C), recommended for rheumatism, for their beneficial effects on skin, and for much more besides. The surroundings are spectacular: from the medieval village of Montemerano (heavily influenced by the omnipresent Aldobrandeschi family) to Manciano, an agricultural centre overlooked by a monumental 15th century fortress and enriched by the Museo di Preistoria e Protostoria (Museum of Prehistory and Early History) of Valle del Fiora, whose exhibits document the presence of man in the area right back from the Copper and Bronze Ages. Proceeding along the regional road n. 74 ("Maremmana") for less than twenty kilometres, travellers will come upon the architectural miracle of Pitigliano, a village that takes shape on a spur of tufa rock overhanging the valley. Strolling through the narrow streets and exploring the Etruscan tombs that today serve as cellars, one comes upon the Jewish Ghetto whose fame was to lend Pitigliano the name of 'Little Jerusalem', with its synagogue, library packed with ancient texts, and cemetery.

THE EXPERIMENT OF NOMADELFIA

"If it were to take a thousand years to develop a fraternal civilization, then we would need to prepare by loving and feeling close those who will live a thousand years from now." These are the words of Zeno Saltini, a priest who, after the war, founded a community in which there is no private property, and no money circulates, where there are no careers, and where all adults are fathers and mothers to all children. After several mishaps, in the 1950s Nomadelfia found its permanent location a few kilometres away from Grosseto, between the villages

Above, Pitigliano.
Right, Girifalco in Piazza del Duomo.

of Roselle and Batignano, in an stretch of land that, over the years, the members of the community have reclaimed and made fertile. Visited in 1989 by Pope John Paul II, and taken as the subject for a television drama, Nomadelfia defines itself "a proposal", offering a concrete, tangible sign that living together in peace as brothers and sisters is possible. The community, which demonstrates that such living is possible in Tuscany, takes in and provides accommodation to visitors.

BALESTRO DEL GIRIFALCO

It is not just a shooting contest. The Balestro del Girifalco, scheduled for the fourth Sunday in May and the second Sunday in August in Massa Marittima (close to the metal-bearing hills of Grosseto), is a magnificent medieval re-enactment including over one hundred and fifty flag bearers, musicians and participants in medieval costume. The event takes place in the 13th century Piazza Garibaldi, in front of the Cathedral, which houses one of the most famous "Maestà" (Madonna enthroned holding the infant Jesus) by Duccio di Buoninsegna (1255-1318), the founder of the Sienese school of painting.

SIENA

Piazza del Campo, Siena.

> When once you have seen the Mangia,
> all other towers, obelisks, and columns
> are tame and vulgar and earth-rooted;
> that seems to quit the ground,
> to be not a monument but a flight.
>
> *William Dean Howells*

THE PIAZZA

Siena, the epitome of the medieval city-state and a city with a glorious culture and past, is located in the exact centre of Tuscany. The town invariably evokes nostalgia in those who visit. It leaves a languid stupor that has a precise colour: that "sienna" that floods the rooftops, the façades and the memories of all who have been. Its black and white Cathedral, a treasure trove of masterpieces, and its Baptistery, with the baptismal font designed by Jacopo della Quercia and Donatello, would be sufficient to make it an unforgettable destination. Yet, its centre of gravity is elsewhere, some four hundred yards away, down Via di Stalloreggi and Via di Città. The Piazza del Campo is the perfect meeting place even if you are halfway around the world. Anyone knows how to get there, and all of Siena flows into this 'shell', serving as the city's nerve centre for the past seven hundred years. In the evening, it is transformed into a magical, multi-ethnic *chaise longue:* sitting or lying down on its herringbone brickwork, and looking up at the 14th century Torre del Mangia that stands proud over the Palazzo Pubblico, conveys a thrill that will not fade with time. "If God had a voice, it would be very similar to that of Bocelli," said Celine Dion some years ago. And if He chose an earthly abode, He would probably opt for Siena.

VIA FRANCIGENA

Via Francigena is a one hundred kilometre route crossing right through the province, and indeed Tuscany as a whole, to be covered on foot, on horseback, by bicycle or by car. This mystical, commercial and cultural artery of Europe once sparked, especially during the Romanesque period, an unprecedented architectural development of fortified structures, churches and abbeys.

Among the places touched by the *via peregrinalis* par excellence (an axis connecting the Holy Land, Rome and Compostela), most worthy of note are San Gimignano, a miracle of medieval town planning, with its fifteen towers, and Monteriggioni, a raised mirage that moves the clock back eight hundred years. Beyond Siena, the route reaches the great cypress-lined abbey of Monte Oliveto, a treasure trove of masterpieces and ancient texts, and

then Buonconvento, before entering the moon-like landscape of the Crete Senesi district. Nearby are the "ideal" Renaissance city of Pienza, the splendid 13th century abbey of Sant'Antimo, the thermal baths, known since Roman times, of Bagno Vignoni (in a province that offers many places renowned for their healing waters, from Chianciano to Rapolano and Petriolo), and Radicofani, offering a birds eye view encompassing Tuscany, Lazio and Umbria.

A FESTIVE SKIRMISH

"The Palio is the Palio. No sociological, historical or anthropological interpretation could ever explain it. It is at once the sublimation and damnation of those fated to come from Siena." Thus the poet Mario Luzi describes the frenzied, wonderful horse race that every person from Siena eagerly awaits the whole year round and that would appear to end after just three laps of the Piazza del Campo.

Tourists, international cameras, foreign commentators are intrusions that the inhabitants politely tolerate. But the Palio is their affair. And a very serious affair it

Above: aerial view of San Gimignano. Left, Via Francigena.

Top, Allegory of Good Government.
Palazzo Pubblico, Siena.
Above, The Palio of Siena.

is, mixing the sacred and the profane. It has its roots in the Middle Ages, and stills arouses an unimaginable tumult of passions at every edition.

Twice a year (July 2nd and August 16th) the outer perimeter of the square is covered with a layer of tufa, transforming it into a racecourse, home to a bareback horse race. Ten participants represent as many districts, or Contradas, randomly selected among the seventeen situated within the medieval walls: districts

experienced, by those who live there, as an extension of their own home. Beyond the magnificent historical procession, with its six hundred participants and flag bearers in medieval costume, beyond the frenzied race that attracts anyone who watches, the Palio is even more fascinating before and after the actual event: the practice runs leading up to the race, the songs of the Contrada men, the good wishes, the verbal wars, the blessing of the horses in church, the dinner on the eve of the race, that turns the Contradas into huge open-air restaurants, the raillery against the losers, the weeping of the runners-up (the utmost dishonour), and the celebrations in honour of he who wins the "Cencio", or rag, a painted cloth in itself of modest value, but symbolically priceless.

SIENESE SCHOOL OF PAINTING

The Sienese School of painting flourished in Siena between the 13th and 15th centuries and for a time rivalled Florence. Its most important exponent was Duccio di Buoninsegna (the leader of the movement), whose work shows a Byzantine influence, reinterpreted in the light of the latest trends in Gothic art. His monumental altarpiece in the Cathedral of Siena, completed in 1311, depicts the Enthroned Madonna and Child. Other leading names of the "school" are Pietro and Ambrogio Lorenzetti and Simone Martini. In terms of sculpture, Jacopo della Quercia (Siena, c. 1374 - Siena, 1438) is particularly worthy of note. His is the Fonte Gaia, or rectangular marble basin, situated in the Piazza del Campo. The

Abbey of Sant'Antimo.

original can be seen in the museum complex of the ancient Ospedale di Siena, in Piazza del Duomo.

A CONTRADA MAN DEVOTED TO OPERA

Of bronze and velvet: so music lovers describe the voice of Ettore Bastianini (1922-1967), a great baritone and a passionate Contrada man. His was a short life, tragic and mocking, just like that of the characters he played, alongside singers of the calibre of Maria Callas, Giacomo Lauri Volpi and Jussi Bjorling. The destitute son of an unknown father, he was able to develop his amazing voice thanks to the teachings of Luciano Bettarini, the same Master who decades later pitched the voice of Andrea Bocelli. At the age of forty, Bastianini discovered he had throat cancer. He kept the news hidden even from his partner, with whom he then broke up. Captain of the Panther Contrada, he celebrated its success at the Palio of July 2nd, 1963. When he died four years later, all of Siena turned out for the last rites. As the funeral procession passed in front of the Piazza del Campo, his coffin was turned to face the Torre del Mangia, as the bell of the Palazzo Comunale sounded the death knell. Today, a road of his native Contrada bears his name.

THE ART OF COOKING

Stale bread soaked in water... destined for the rubbish heap, you might think.. And you'd be wrong. In Tuscany it is dried in a cloth, crumbled, and seasoned with olive oil, vinegar, salt and pepper. To this are added tomatoes, chopped onion and basil, to make the "panzanella", a typical example of humble, healthy and delicious Sienese cooking. Other savoury dishes include bean soup served with slices of toasted garlic bread, and "pici", delicious handmade spaghetti topped with Cacio cheese and pepper, or with a spicy and highly garlicky tomato sauce. It is with its desserts, however, that the gastronomic tradition of Siena reaches its peak. Particularly worthy of note are: the Ricciarelli biscuits, made with a coarse marzipan paste enriched with vanilla and candied fruit, rolled into the shape of a large, rough grain of rice; "Panforte", an ancient cake made with nuts, almonds and candied fruit; and "Panpepato", flavoured with honey, pepper, almonds and nutmeg. Not to mention that Siena contends with the city of Treviso for the right to lay first claim on the world-renowned "tiramisu".

Left, laneways in Siena. Above, Panforte and Panzanella.

Cypress trees adorning the rolling Sienese hills.

TWO WHEELS

The gentleness of the land surrounding Siena and the intensity of its olfactory, visual and auditory experiences are an invitation to cycle. An intricate system of trails and services enables two-wheeled travellers to visit every corner of the province, from Chianti to Val d'Elsa, from Siena to the Crete Senesi district, from Val di Merse to Val d'Orcia, from Val di Chiana to Mount Amiata, with routes suited to every skill level.

Furthermore, it is possible to join excursions on 'Littorina' railcars, setting off from Siena for fairs, feasts and festivals. After a bracing bike trail, well-being enthusiasts can avail of one of the many spas in the province of Siena, including the aforementioned centres of Chianciano, Rapolano and Bagno Vignoni.

BRUNELLO

The name of Montalcino, a town with five thousand inhabitants, standing five hundred meters above sea level (a sea of rolling hills, chequered with fields, olive groves and vineyards, and overlooked by the town's 14th century fortress), is inextricably linked with a wine with an exceptional lingering aroma: the "Brunello".

In the beginning it was a white wine: indeed, in the 1600s the local "moscadello" grape was much appreciated. In the late 1800s the vine-grower Ferruccio Biondi Santi, upon returning from Garibaldi's campaigns to unite Italy, decided to devote himself to one variety, the "Sangiovese Grosso" (or "Brunello").

Brunello wine, if well-preserved, has an exceptionally long life. Indeed, late 19th century specimens have recently been uncorked at elite tastings. This ruby-coloured wine spends four years in oak barrels before being bottled, its alcohol content reaching 13.5 percent. Because after all, as Goethe teaches us, "Life's too short to drink bad wines."

SAN GALGANO

The sky serves as the roof of the abbey devoted to Saint Galgano, just as the sky fills its rose window, and below, the two orders of mullioned windows of the apse. The Abbazia di San Galgano is a giant wound to Christianity. Its very lesions have given it an evocative power that makes it unique in the world. In a soft green valley in the hills of Chiusdino, some thirty kilometres from Siena, stands a 13th century complex comprising the Eremo di Montesiepi (Monastery of Montesiepi) and an abbey with a Latin cross plan. The decline of San Galgano, brought about by pestilence, lightning, and various raids (its lead facing was sold to make bullets), led to its deconsecration in the 18th century. In the summer, the abbey is transformed into an 800-seat theatre hosting plays, operas and ballets. However, the best music to be heard here is silence, or at most the sounds of nature, when, in the early hours of the morning, the majestic Cistercian Gothic-inspired ruins reveal their mystical vocation as a corridor between the earth, with its inhabitants, and the sky, with its inhabitants.

Montalcino.

For me, life is often a harmonious balance of extreme feelings. There are moments of calm, when everything is as quiet as when the snow falls gently to the ground, and others of great turmoil, when passion necessarily rages... Siena well represents the balance between these opposites, with the magnificent perfection of its architecture, the impetuosity of its Palio, and the silent wonder of its surrounding countryside.

Andrea Bocelli

THE SWORD IN THE STONE

Could the original Round Table be concealed in the hills of Siena? Canonised in 1185, Saint Galgano was a medieval knight turned hermit after whom the famous Abbazia di San Galgano and, nearby, a monastery and a chapel in the Romanesque style have been named. This monastery still preserves the sword that the saint plunged into the rock to show his will to change his life, turning it into a Christian symbol. A somewhat controversial and fascinating theory argues that the Tuscany Excalibur pre-dates the British one, and that the poems on the Holy Grail are the fruit of a Persian reworking of the stories of the Three Kings, which arrived in Europe around the 12th century, were contaminated, upon reaching Italy, by the figure of Galgano (renamed Parsifal), and were then developed by Chrétien de Troyes at the court of Aquitaine.

Abbey of San Galgano.

CHIANTI

Beauty rarely coincides with perfection. And yet, the hills of the Chianti region, inhabited for four thousand years, are the exception that proves the rule. Set between the Arno basin, south of Florence, and the province of Siena, lie the unstable and contested boundaries of a place that has become a world icon of quality of life and bounty of nature. It is a book of dreams that we have all, perhaps unconsciously, leafed through. So much so that a visit to Chianti means "rediscovering" rather than "discovering", finding that ideal land that we carry within ourselves. The hills roll with the visual rhythm of a slow waltz, through vineyards, olive groves, oaks, chestnuts, pines, shrubs and herb plants. This is a holy land, with its countless time-worn churches, and a turreted land, with castles and fortifications (and wineries, and farms) that have lost their aggressive venom, now redolent of fairy tales and legends. Just think of Radda, with its Palazzo Pretorio, and Gaiole, Castellina, Greve... But there would be no point drawing up a priority of places to visit. Here, one could choose the route to take, at every crossroads, with one's eyes closed. And here, many prominent personalities, often foreigners, have found their permanent shelter. Chianti is, notoriously, the wine heart of Tuscany. It is the birthplace of the world's most famous Italian wine, resulting from an expert blend of Sangiovese, Canaiolo, Malvasia and Trebbiano grapes. The age-old custom of cultivating different varieties in the same vineyard creates, in autumn, a range of colours to which no pen could ever do justice.

FIRENZE
Florence

Panoramic view of Florence with the Cathedral Santa Maria del Fiore, Giotto's bell tower and Palazzo Vecchio.

The twenty years I spent in Florence were the most important of my life. It was there that I discovered that, besides the sea, there is also terra firma
- the terra firma of ideas, tradition, humanism. There I found a different nature, one that pervades man's worth and thought. It was there that I learned what civilization has been and can be.

Eugenio Montale

...The longer you live there and the more you realise you love the city.
There is something so welcoming as to make me feel at home.

Pëtr Il'ič Čajkovskij

THE DESTINATION

Florence is a dangerous place: it has and is everything a traveller could want. In this it is disconcerting, just as entering the British Library can be disconcerting for an avid reader.

It is impossible to get to know Florence in its entirety, unless you are planning on taking a sabbatical year (and perhaps even that wouldn't be enough).

The short cut we propose is a far cry from the usual cram-packed tour that sets out to see "as much as possible" (which, in any case, is always just the tip of the iceberg), and warns visitors against that tourist bulimia that starts with the best of intentions, but often - and paradoxically - leaves a feeling of dissatisfaction.

The cradle of art, the mother of the Italian language, the home of opera ... To enjoy Florence to the full, to understand it, one must experience it for what it is: an all-

absorbing emotional experience requiring a nose dive into a new element, with the utmost joy and with one's senses fully alert. One must "swim" with slow strokes towards a fictitious goal, because water has no route; because each single step is a destination in itself.

Only then, whether for a day a week or month, wherever you have come from, you can hope to be a true citizen of the art capital of the world. Only then can you consider yourself Florentine.

TOO BEAUTIFUL?

"I had reached that stage of excitement where one feels the heavenly sensations granted by the Arts and one's most passionate feelings. As I emerged from the porch of Santa Croce, I was seized with a fierce palpitation of the heart; the well-spring of life was dried up within me, and I walked in constant fear of falling to the ground." So Stendhal wrote in the passage that inaugurated the famous syndrome named after the author, also known as the "syndrome of Florence": dizziness, before so much, and such extraordinary magnificence. The Cathedral and its dome, the Baptistery of San Giovanni, Giotto's bell tower, the Palazzo Vecchio, Ponte Vecchio, Piazza della Signoria, Michelangelo's David,

Top left, ancient music scores. Above, The Uffizi, in the evening.

the Uffizi Gallery, Palazzo Pitti, the Galleria dell'Accademia, the Galleria Palatina, Santa Croce, Santa Maria Novella, San Miniato, San Lorenzo, masterpieces by Donatello, Botticelli, Brunelleschi, Masaccio, Michelangelo... Florence is all this and much more. But do not be daunted by such a wealth of wonders: what's important is to select, dilute, perhaps even put off. The figure of speech known as synecdoche (in which a part is substituted for a whole) perfectly describes the short cut mentioned above: because, in any case, there's nothing more certain than that you will, one day, return to Florence. And so you might as well slow down, choose routes off the beaten track, discover - for every "must see" - one or two works of art far, from the madding crowds and the canonical tourist itineraries. The key word is, be prepared to be surprised. Live the city to the full, in first person, with its colours, its food, its shop windows, its most hidden corners, its walks, without the anxiety of missing out on a must (because everything here is a must).

AN EMOTIVE GUIDE

The "Voice of Tuscany" to be strummed in your heart on approaching the city, could have the seductive and passionate pace of Lauretta's aria "Oh, my dear papa", from the opera *Gianni Schicchi* by Puccini. Memorise the soundtrack and let it dictate the rhythm of your steps and glances. The plot - ironic, sharp, yet indulgent (like the people of Tuscany) - was inspired by a passage from the *Inferno,* the first part of the *Divine Comedy* penned by Dante Alighieri, the Florentine poet considered the father of the Italian language (the Casa di Dante Museum - Dante's house - lies in the heart of the old city, in Via Santa Margherita). Florence serves as the backdrop for Puccini's opera, which makes many references to the city's history, landscape and architecture, with precise geographical indications and a phrase book full of local expressions.
The declaration of love, plea for help, request for a ring, and threat of a reckless act (not very credibly, she threatens to throw herself from the Ponte Vecchio), sung by a daughter in love, in a melody with a tempo that is "andante sostenuto", can help to synchronise your senses to the flow of the River Arno and to the lyrical outpouring of the city that accompanies its bends.

Bottom, ancient books for sale at the flee market and a flower stand. Right: Basilica of Santa Maria Novella, Florence.

WHEN EATING MEANS UNDERSTANDING

In the words of Andrea Bocelli, the "lampredotto", named for its resemblance to the lamprey eel, once very abundant in the waters of the River Arno, is a delicacy both "humble and tasty". Although not a dish for tourists, being somewhat of an acquired taste, it helps those who savour it to understand the popular and ancient local cuisine (and with it, as often happens, to understand the land and its people). The Florentine cuisine offers many specialities, from appetisers based on cold meats and crostini, to bread soup, the "Fiorentina" (a sandwich, with the bread partially soaked in broth, or "in zimino", in other words stewed with chard.

OPERA

Opera as we know it was born in Via de' Benci, in the historical centre of Florence. Here, a group of nobles would meet during the last quarter of the 16th century, at a creative workshop in the home of Count Giovanni Bardi, to discuss music, literature and science. The "Camerata de 'Bardi", as it was known, included members such as Vincenzo Galilei (Galileo Galilei's father), Jacopo Peri, Giulio Caccini and Ottavio

Left, street in Florence. Above, Castagnaccio and Spices.

grilled T-bone steak served rare), baccalà (dried cod), and a typical chocolate cake. But the lampredotto is more visceral, both figuratively and literally speaking: the "Florentine tripe" - cow's stomach slow boiled with tomatoes, onions, celery, parsley and various herbs - can be eaten with a green sauce, made with parsley, anchovies and capers, or, chopped, as a stuffing for round bread rolls. Even today, many "lampredottai" sell the traditional lampredotto from their kiosks scattered around Florence, either as a "moist"

Rinuccini. The aim of Count Bardi was to revive the classical Greek tragedy, in contrast with the polyphonic madrigal, and make room for "recitar cantando" (acting through song) and instrumentally-accompanied monodies, giving rise to a new, revolutionary concept of musical theatre. Some of the greatest 20th century interpreters of this alchemy of music and drama came from Florence, such as the tenor Mario Del Monaco and the baritones Gino Bechi and Rolando Panerai. The history of music is further indebted

to the city for eminent composers of the calibre of Luigi Cherubini (1760-1842), and for the production - no less - of the piano. The instrument - an evolution of the harpsichord, capable of producing a dynamic sound that can be controlled by the performer - was born around the year 1700, invented by Bartolomeo Cristofori at the Florentine court of Cosimo III de 'Medici. The piano soon became a favourite instrument with the greatest composers of the western world (starting with Haydn, Mozart and Beethoven).

A CITY WAITING TO BE DISCOVERED

In addition to Florence's best known jewels, the city is like a treasure hunt, with prizes to be found at every step of the way. Here, curios, secrets and concealed masterpieces are camouflaged under the frescoed ceilings of shops, on the street flooring, in the decorated walls of ancient trattorias, or in the atriums of private mansions. As for "out of the way" museums, there are plenty to choose from: Veterani e Reduci Giuseppe Garibaldi (with memorabilia of the veterans of Garibaldi's campaigns to unite Italy), in Piazza San Martino; Sport's Museum, in Via Maggio; Museo dell'Istituto Agrario (agricultural museum), in Viale delle Cascine; Museo della Misericordia

Left: the Arno's flow in Florence and Ponte Vecchio. Top, goldsmith in his workshop; a romantic carriage.

di Firenze (with memorabilia of the Florentine Venerabile Arciconfraternita brotherhood), in Piazza Duomo; Casa del Tessuto (fabric museum), in Via dei Pecori; Officina Profumo-Farmaceutica di Santa Maria Novella (perfume and pharmaceutics museum), in Via della Scala; Museo Ferragamo, displaying shoes worn by Greta Garbo and Marilyn Monroe, in Via de' Tornabuoni; and Museo della Specola, with its skeleton hall and "forgotten" rooftop observatory, in Via Romana.

SWEET AND CREATIVE

Florence is not just about opera and the piano, or about the telephone (Antonio Meucci), the "Reason of State" (Niccolò Machiavelli), the adventures of Pinocchio (Carlo Collodi) and the Americas (Amerigo Vespucci). Florence also boasts the discovery of ice cream. Bernardo Buontalenti (1531-1608) was an architect, sculptor and engineer, responsible for the Uffizi and the Villa Medicea in Pratolino. On the occasion of the visit to Florence of a Spanish embassy delegation, Buontalenti is said to have helped the court confectioners to devise new sorbets by inventing a machine, in the shape of a closed box, with an insulating cavity, in which various ingredients (such as milk, eggs, honey, a

drop of wine, snow and a pinch of salt to lower the temperature) would solidify when stirred using spatulas driven by an external handle.

FIESOLE

Fiesole is a hilltop town much beloved by Giovanni Boccaccio, Marcel Proust, Gertrude Stein and Hermann Hesse. Home to one of the least known and best preserved Medici villas, Fiesole was once a strategic crossroads, and is now an attractive landmark of Tuscany. The town, surrounded by olive groves and punctuated by Renaissance villas, boasts an Etruscan archaeological site of great importance, situated less than ten kilometres away from Florence. The site includes a well-preserved Roman amphitheatre from the 1st century BC (home, in the summer, to many concerts and shows), the remains of an Etruscan temple, and baths from the Augustan age, as well as an archaeological museum. On the first Sunday of every month, an antiques market is held in Piazza Mino da Fiesole, the square where the town's imposing Romanesque cathedral devoted to St. Romulus stands. On top of the hill stands a 14th century Franciscan Monastery, from which one can enjoy one of the most breathtaking views of Florence. The Parco di Monteceneri, near Fiesole, features the hill used by Leonardo da Vinci to test his flying machine in 1506.
Here, there is also a pedestrian route through the old quarries of Maiano, famous for their sandstone, the so-called "pietra fiesolana", commonly used by sculptors since the 15th century.

THE LAND OF LEONARDO

At once a painter, sculptor, inventor, architect, engineer and scientist, Leonardo (son of Piero da Vinci) is perhaps the most diversely talented person ever to have lived. His spirit permeates Vinci, the town where he was born in 1452. The village, on the slopes of Montalbano (thirty kilometres from Florence), hosts the Biblioteca Leonardiana and the Museo Leonardiano, situated in the Palazzina Uzielli and the Castello dei Conti Guidi (the latter in itself an architectural masterpiece, often referred to as the "ship-like castle"

Above, The Vitruvian Man by Leonardo, wooden sculpture. Left, Museo Leonardiano, Vinci.

due to its shape), housing a large collection of machines and models developed by Leonardo the inventor, technologist and engineer. Other sites dedicated to the author of the *Mona Lisa* include the Museo Ideale Leonardo da Vinci, which celebrates the master's universal genius, and the home where he was born, in the village of Anchiano.

LITERARY WALKS

Marradi, in the Mugello Valley, bordering with the region of Emilia Romagna, is set in a hilly landscape of oaks, beeches

> *If ever I feel depressed, I go back to Florence and look at Brunelleschi's Dome: if man can achieve such wonders, then I can and must try to create, do, live.*
> Franco Zeffirelli

> *Florence is a city that revives hope.*
> Andrej Tarkovsky

and chestnut trees. The town's palaces tell of an illustrious past as an important crossroads. Dino Campana (1885-1932), one of the greatest Italian poets of the 20th century, was born in these lands, with which he had a love-hate relationship and through which he wandered extensively, in a sort of vagrancy, celebrating the area in his verses. The author of *Orphic Songs* describes the "rocks, forming layer upon layer" of the streams, the railway of Faenza, inaugurated in 1893, the bridge over the River Lamone (which crosses Marradi), mentioned in one of his most famous poems, and "La Colombaia", from which he would observe the "Triangolo del Castellone" and the red dome of Marradi's Town Hall. There are many literary trails starting at Marradi and bound for the Apennine ridge.

The town also lends its name to the "Marradi chestnut" (celebrated at the traditional Chestnut Festival that takes place every Sunday in October), an important ingredient of both sweet and savoury local dishes, including chestnut ravioli, chestnut cake, castagnaccio and *marrons glacés*.

Landscape in the Mugello Valley.

> *Fertile valleys of the Valdichiana from the Tiber to the Arno with the mountains of the Casentino in the background, still preserving the glory of its antiquity under its simple appearance. Arezzo.*
>
> Gabriele D'Annunzio

THE CLASSIC CITY

A small central zone in innermost Tuscany, a place thousands of years old, Etruscan, then Roman, then Medieval (the historical epoch that still today characterises the city), a pulsing heart of beauty dressed in the four valleys that extend the province: Casentino, Valdichiana, Valdarno and Valtiberina...

Arezzo has transformed and renewed itself over the centuries, sowing works of art and noble sons, from the Benedictine monk, Guido – who in the early eleventh century invented modern musical notation and named the seven notes – to the 14th century poet Petrarch, the painter and architect Giorgio Vasari and the poet Pietro Aretino.

Developed along a slope, the city offers a historic centre teeming with masterpieces, from the Gothic cathedral (which dominates the urban fabric) to the Romanesque parish church of Santa Maria, the medieval church of San Domenico, on the altar of which stands a superb crucifix by Cimabue, and the church of San Francesco, which preserves the *Legend of the True Cross* fresco cycle by Piero della Francesca, one of the pictorial peaks of the 15th century. Capital of the goldsmith's art and antiques

Piazza Grande, Arezzo.

Above, The joust of the"Saracen". Right, Loggia di Vasari.

(the latter being the focus of a famed market held in the Piazza Grande the first weekend of every month), it is a city of museums (from the Diocesano, next to the Cathedral, to the Museo d'Arte Medievale e Moderna). Arezzo, a city-republic for many centuries, expresses its civilisation through its historic sites of power, from the Palazzo Comunale to the Palazzo Pretorio and from the Fortezza Medicea – a fortress with a star-shaped plan, fortified by ramparts – to the Renaissance loggias designed by Vasari. The house of the latter, which he himself decorated, is open to visitors, as is the birth house of Petrarch.

THE JOUST OF THE SARACEN
Dante Alighieri spoke of it in the Divine Comedy: the Joust of the Saracen, a knightly game with roots in the Middle Ages, ritualising war training drills and simulating battle. The dummy to be dealt a death blow is what was historically once the enemy par excellence of the Christian West: the Arab 'infidel' (the 'Saracen').

Lost during the 18th century, it reappeared at the end of the same century only to disappear again over the course of the nineteenth. The tournament was definitively revived in the 1930s, in a jubilation of medieval costume, flag-wavers, squires and crossbowmen. It is held in the space ringed by the tower houses of the Piazza Grande, by night on the second-to-last Saturday in June (Giostra di San Donato) and by day on the first Sunday of September. The "Saracen" is a wooden bust. On its left arm, a steel plate; on its right, a cat-o'-three-tails with balls of lead and leather. Each of the four participating Arezzo districts is represented by a knight who, armed with a lance, must strike the steel plate while at the same time avoiding getting hit by the three lead balls.

THE CASENTINO
Those longing for the beauty, the silence and the pristine spaces of one of the oldest forests in Europe can go up the River Arno to the lands where the river

Romanesque parish church of Santa Maria.

originates to discover the profound grace of the Casentino Valley. Crossed over the centuries – without being ruined – by Hannibal's armies, the Gauls, the Lombards and the Byzantines, it is a place loaded with memories and wisdom. Wisdom that reverberates in respect for and protection of nature as well as in local artisan and wine and food traditions. The 'Parco Nazionale delle Foreste Casentinesi, Monte Falterona e Campigna' offers priceless chromatic scenery, with centuries-old fir trees and forests of beech and sycamore, chestnut, linden and ash. In a sanctuary immersed in 700 kilometres of green in the Apennines of Tuscany-Romagna, along ancient communication trenches and stone bridges, it is easy to glimpse – softened by the milky fog that often blocks out the panorama – Romanesque churches, medieval castles and monasteries, but also roe deer, stags, wild boar and wolves, the princes of Apennine predators.

SACRED CAMALDOLI

Dating back a thousand years and situated over a thousand metres above sea level, the Benedictine monastic complex of Camaldoli, amidst a forest of firs in the National Park, is divided into two staggered cores (three kilometres away from one another): the Hermitage and the Monastery. In the church of the latter, one finds valuable works of art, including seven 16th century panels by Giorgio Vasari, the same painter, art historian and architect who designed the Uffizi in Florence. In a pharmacy located next to the religious structure one can purchase products made from medicinal herbs as well as honey and oil. Dedicated from the onset to hospitality – one of the rules of Saint Benedict, father of western monasticism – the complex has welcomed popes, princes, politicians and pilgrims. It is in this charismatic place of cultural and political character that, in 1943, the *Codice di Camaldoli* was written, a document conceived by young Christian forces that mapped out the guidelines for the Christian Democratic Party, which would be the leading party of the Italian government for decades.

LAND OF CASTLES

Poppi looks out over the Castentino Valley through a turreted palazzo architecturally similar to the Palazzo

Bottom, forest in Campigna and a glimpse of the Casentino Valley. Right, Ceiling, Monastery of Camaldoli.

Vecchio in Florence. The place, celebrated for its impressive Castello dei Conti Guidi (reachable via Strada Statale 70, Consuma Pass) dominates a territory in which two further such edificies are visible to the naked eye: the Castello di Romena, formerly a 13th century prison and later the love nest of the poet Gabriele D'Annunzio and the actress Eleonora Duse, and the Castello di Porciano, which today hosts the Museo Contadino. Known for the manufacture of organ pipes and its zoo, the village

of Poppi – a stone's throw from the site of the bloody battle of Campaldino in 1289, fought between the Guelphs and Ghibellines – also ties its fame to the important Biblioteca Rilliana, a treasure trove of rare medieval manuscripts and early printed books. Tinging the Castello dei Conti with darkness and curiosity is the legend of the countess Telda, a young and beautiful 14th century window whose custom was to ensnare young lovers at night, only to make them disappear with bloody traps. In the end it was she who was locked up in her tower (called "the tower of the devil") and left to die of hunger.

VALDICHIANA BY BICYCLE

Sixty-two kilometres by bicycle, on the roads of cheese, fruit, oil, wine and Chianina cattle: it is the bicycle path of Arezzo, ending at Chiusi and travelling along the Canale Maestro della Chiana, an artificial water flow realised in the 18th and 19th century in the southernmost portion of the province. Perfect for family tourism since relatively flat with only slight differences of level (20 metres in total), this ancient road, built for the maintenance of the sluices and the canal, accompanies

us in the heart of Etruscan civilisation through dreamy landscapes, oil mills, artisan bottegas and urban gems such as Castiglion Fiorentino, the fortified village of Lucignano with its elliptical shape and concentric roads, or Monte San Savino, the "city of wine" and art ceramics. Special services are available for the bicycle tourist, including bicycle rentals for every need, minibus or guide assistance and the option to follow the route by the train.

CORTONA AND ITS LAUD BOOK

Cortona's winding roads, through natural terracings that dominate the Valdichiana, hold the oldest testimony

Above, two glimpses of the Castello dei Conti Guidi in Poppi.
Right, Church of Santa Maria Nuova in Val di Chiana.

tied to the birth of Italian melody: the thirteenth-century Laud Book that bears that name of the town, gathering forty-seven pieces (accompanied by musical notation) dedicated to the Madonna and to liturgical feasts. In addition to religious architecture from various centuries (from the 15th century church of San Domenico to the Cathedral, reconstructed in the 18th century), Cortona offers the visitor the treasures of the Museo Diocesano (which houses works by Luca Signorelli and a magnificent *Annunciation* by Beato Angelico, also known as Fra Angelico), as well as those of the MAEC, an Etruscan museum avant-garde for the services it offers, also to the blind, through dozens of tactile prototypes.

TERRACOTTA

For more than one hundred years, between the 15th and 16th century,

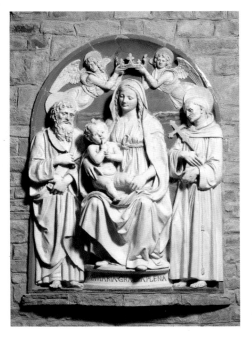

the Della Robbia family beautified the world using the technique of glazed polychrome terracotta. Starting with Luca Della Robbia, the inventor of the process (discovered around 1440), this dynasty of sculptors from Tuscany passed down the technique, applying it to the plasticity of sacred subjects but also to heraldic coats of arms. Blue and ivory, the characteristic colours of the Della Robbia workshop majolica, produced through a process parallel to that of fossilisation, map out the geography of the Arezzo province, translating today into an ideal touristic route. In Valtiberina, one travels from the splendid medieval village of Anghiari, with an altarpiece of the Madonna della Misericordia (Madonna of Mercy) in the church of Santa Maria delle Grazie, to Sansepolcro, where one finds a *Nativity* in the Museo Civico. In Valdichiana one can admire the *Crucifixion with mourners and saints* in the church of San Francesco in Foiano. Monte San Savino also preserves celebrated glazed Della Robbia terracottas (in the church of Santa Chiara), as do Castiglion Fiorentino and Cortona.
In Valdarno, the art of the Della Robbia has left a major mark, from Montevarchi to Bucine as well as the Casentino Valley, where around fifty Della Robbia works are distributed among places tied to Camaldolese and Franciscan spirituality. The tour can be completed in the capital, Arezzo, with the extraordinary pieces on view in the Cathedral, the Museo Ivan Bruschi, Santa Maria in Gradi and the Museo Diocesano.

Above, panoramic view of Cortona. Left, Glazed terracotta.

> Man was created for living here, where, with the toil of his labour in the fields, he can procure everything that he needs for a tranquil life and where he can also meditate on the profound meaning and spiritual value of his time spent on earth safe from the contradictions, vices, absurdities and tensions of the increasingly oppressive reinforced concrete world, where saying triumphs over doing, having over being, the frivolous over the useful, and the superficial over the concrete.
>
> *Andrea Bocelli*

CAPRESE MICHELANGELO

According to legend, Totila (a name which means "the immortal" in the language of the Goths), king of the Ostrogoths, died here in 552. What is certain is that in this little place nestled amongst the chestnut groves of the Valtiberina, the Renaissance was born. The son of the town's podestà, Michelangelo Buonarroti - a restless apostle of beauty - was born here in 1475: after the genius behind the *David* and the fresco cycle on the ceiling of the Sistine Chapel, western art would never be the same. The Palazzo del Podestà, the birth house of the artist, is one of the centres of the Museo Michelangiolesco, together with the Palazzo Clusini, the Corte Alta and an open-air exhibition centre, which house life-size reproductions of the sculptor and painter's celebrated masterpieces, as well as a substantial collection of contemporary works.

THE LANDSCAPES OF PIERO DELLA FRANCESCA

The ploughed fields, holm oak hills, rocky mountains and dazzling nature of easternmost Tuscany (diagonally

Above, Piero Della Francesca, the Mystery of the True Cross. Left, Sansepolcro.

crossed by the Tiber, the river "soul" of Rome), find striking references in the backgrounds of the works of Piero della Francesca, master of colour, light and perspective. The great painter-humanist of the Renaissance was born around 1416 in Sansepolcro, a town not to be missed for its churches, 15th century buildings, goldsmiths and above all the Museo Civico (inside the 14th century Palazzo dei Conservatori), which houses four of the artist's most celebrated works: the *Resurrection*, the polyptych of the *Madonna of Mercy* and paintings

representing Saint Julian and Saint Louis, as well as works by Pontormo, Della Robbia and Signorelli. The itinerary can be continued toward Monterchi, the birthplace of the artist's mother, a village near the Umbria border where della Francesca produced the *Madonna del Parto*, an image revolutionary for its expression of "human" rather than divine intensity. Final stop, the Basilica of San Francesco in Arezzo, where the Bacci Chapel hosts the above-mentioned fresco cycle of the *Legend of the True Cross*.

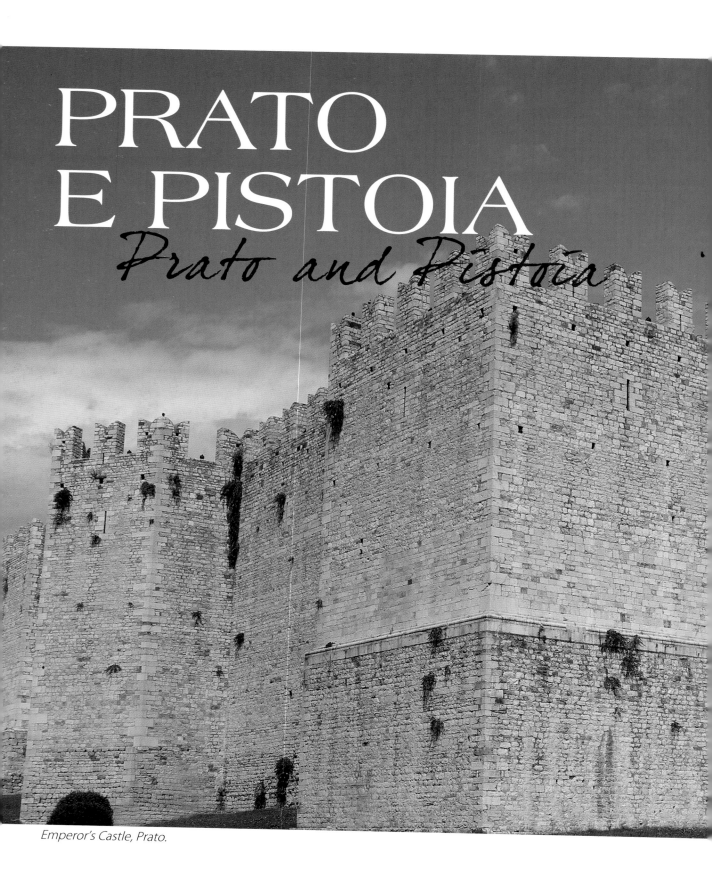

PRATO E PISTOIA
Prato and Pistoia

Emperor's Castle, Prato.

PRATO, ANCIENT AND MODERN

If you were to stretch a piece of string between Florence and Pistoia, Prato would be exactly in the middle, about twenty kilometres from both. The second city of Tuscany, it is not only a populous, hard-working industrial centre with a historical predilection for textiles. Prato is also a place with thousands of years of history that relies on a formidable artistic culture and tourist industry, as confirmed by a dense calendar of events. Located in the valley of the Bisenzio River, a thousand years ago Prato was already a strategic commercial junction: it is no coinci dence that in the middle of the 13th century Frederick II of Swabia built an imposing castle here (known as the "Castello dell'Imperatore", or Emperor's Castle) to control the communication roads that led to Germany from the south. The historic centre is filled with a wealth of examples of medieval architecture, like the Cathedral and the Palazzo Pretorio, as well as the intact sections of the city wall and the restored "Cassero", a fortified communication trench that connects the walls near the Porta Fiorentina with the castle interior. Its identity as an ancient city looking to the future is well illustrated by the presence, in the south east periphery, of the Centro per l'Arte Contemporanea Luigi Pecci, one of the most prestigious exhibition centres in Europe. The Prato territory offers superb examples of Medici architecture, including the Villa di Poggio in Caiano (perhaps the design masterpiece among those commissioned by Lorenzo the Magnificent), "La Ferdinanda" in the medieval village of Artimino, also known as "the villa of the hundred chimneys", and the site of the Museo Archeologico Comunale.

A BILINGUAL CITY

Prato hosts the third largest Chinese community in Europe, after London and Paris. Coming mostly from the province of Zhejiang, it is estimated that here the Chinese represent one tenth of the population. Tangible evidence is seen in the bilingual signs posted at many shops. The Asian presence is tied to the fact that the industrial district surrounding the city is home to one of the most conspicuous concentrations of textile activity in the old continent: businesses specialised in the production of textiles for clothing, yarn for knitwear and fabric articles for footwear and furnishings. In many cases you can do some shopping – at highly competitive prices – right inside the factories. In the centre of Prato, the Museo del Tessuto occupies a historic

shearing shop (a gem of 18th century industrial architecture) and expresses the memory of an industry that the territory has been dedicated to for more than eight centuries.

AN OPERATIC AND LITERARY HOTHOUSE

Among the singers who walked through the door of his house on Via Magnolfi are Fedora Barbieri, Ferruccio Tagliavini, Franco Corelli, Rolando Panerai, Ettore Bastianini and Andrea Bocelli. An orchestra director and composer, Luciano Bettarini (1914-1997) wrote a lyric opera dedicated to his beloved Prato. But his name remains tied to his didactic activity, as the Maestro of some of the greatest voices of the twentieth century.

In the literary sphere, we find such exceptional Prato natives as Curzio Malaparte (1898-1957), a writer and author of historic reports from the front lines of European wars, and the playwright Sem Benelli (1877-1949), author of the play *La cena delle beffe*, which enjoyed clamorous success and became a film and a lyric opera by Umberto Giordano.

BISCOTTINI DI PRATO

Among their admirers one finds the German writer Herman Hesse: they are cantucci, but it is better to call them by their true name, especially here, where the recipe was perfected. Biscotti di Prato are biscuits prepared with an abundance of almonds and shaped from a small long log cut diagonally. Their gastronomic marriage with Vin Santo is renowned. But don't fall into the easy trap of dunking them, say the purists. It must be a pairing: eat the one, drink the other.

Herod's banquet, frescoes by Filippo Lippi, in the Cathedral of Prato.

PISTOIA: THE CITY OF WALLS

Marked by the chromatic rhythm of white and green marble, Pistoia - the city of pulpits, and the city of three rings of wall - is an urban gem that offers visitors a trip back through time in its historic centre, which is in good part pedestrian-only. Between churches, cloisters, ancient piazzas, tower houses, small squares and lanes, the city offers a journey through the history of Italian art from the Romanesque to the Renaissance and the Baroque, up to the present day.

In the centre of the first circle of walls, dating to the period of Lombard domination, one finds the ancient beating heart of civic and religious power in Pistoia: the Piazza del Duomo. Here rises the Cathedral of San Zeno with a large white marble arcade embellished with a bas relief by Andrea della Robbia. Inside is the dossal of San Jacopo, a masterpiece of goldwork dedicated to the cult of the patron saint. The octagonal Baptistery is a few metres away, followed by the Palazzo del Comune (inside which one finds the Museo Civico) and the medieval Palazzo dei Vescovi, home of the Museo Tattile, which displays a three-dimensional map of Pistoia's monumental buildings.

Every Wednesday and Saturday, a market fills the Piazza del Duomo and its surrounding streets. The piazza is also the site of summer events, like the Giostra dell'Orso (Tournament of the Bear) held on 25 July, an equestrian re-enactment of the medieval palio in honour of Saint James. Not far off one finds the Piazza della Sala, the city's historic commercial centre, which comes to life every Monday and Saturday thanks to a colourful produce market.

A POET OF URBAN PLANNING

"I was born in Pistoia, in contact with the chestnut groves and in contact with the craftsmen who work the chestnut wood. I was born in a city where, willing or unwillingly, nature remains within": Giovanni Michelucci, whose life spanned an entire century (1891-1990), is a poet of organized space, one of the greatest stars of 20th century architecture. In 1932 he designed the Florence train station, a masterpiece of Italian realism, while in the

Left, Biscottini di Prato; The Pulpit, detail. Above, aerial view of Pistoia.

early 1960s he realised the church of the Autostrada del Sole in Campi Bisenzio. This religious building, with a sail-like shape that catches the eye of every visitor, is located at the crossing of the A11 Firenze-Mare and the Autostrada del Sole motorways, and is a metaphor of the encounter between culture and religion, as well as a symbol of the knocking down of the barriers between north and south. In the Museo Civico of Pistoia, a visit to the Centro di Documentazione Michelucci permits visitors to view the great urban planner's drawings and plans.

A MULTI-SITE MUSEUM

The integration of man with nature is the common denominator of this open-air museum extending along the Pistoia mountains. Six itineraries, six routes made up of places, exhibitions and educational centres together form the Ecomuseo della Montagna Pistoiese. The main information point is in Gavinaga, a village resting on the slopes of Monte Crocicchio. The blue itinerary tours sites of ice production that use river water, winter cold and a system of artificial canals and lakes. An example is the ice house of the Madonnina delle Piastre.
The red 'iron' itinerary, with Pontepetri as its destination, follows the processing of metal coming from the Island of Elba. There are also the violet itinerary, dedicated to religious art (the Museo Diocesano in Popiglio), the yellow, a homage to everyday life (the Museo della Gente di Montagna in Rivoreta) and the green, with the forest botanic garden of Abetone and the archaeological naturalistic centre of Campo Tizzoro.

The Ecomuseo is completed by the grey itinerary, dedicated to the art of quarrying and working stone, in Sambuca Pistoiese.

SPORTS IN VALDINIEVOLE

A great valley between Lucca and Pistoia that mixes pristine landscapes, splendid spa centres, medieval villages and castles: this is Valdinievole, the land of white wines, Vin Santo and a peerless fruity olive oil, and the perfect place for sport vacations, between nature and wellness. Spread throughout the territory are foot paths, parks, gyms, swimming pools, football fields, tennis and basketball courts, boules rinks and horseback riding centres. There are many clubs dedicated to bicycle racing, a sport that can be enjoyed on tracks of every kind, from the most accessible to the most gruelling. For those who love the green, at Monsummano Terme there is an eighteen-hole golf course that follows the conformation of the undulating hills, perfumed with heather, juniper and laurel, and featuring two lakes, a joy for the eyes and the players' thirst for challenge.
At Montecatini Terme one can visit the Sesana racetrack, where the legendary horse Varenne, the fastest trotter of all-time., raced In the environs, there is a trap shooting field that extends for almost half a kilometre.

HEALING WATERS

In the last twenty years of the 19th century, it was not uncommon to glimpse Giuseppe Verdi on its tree-lined avenues. In later decades, Pietro Mascagni, Ruggero Leoncavallo,

Above, Montecatini Terme.
Left, Monsummano Terme.

Beniamino Gigli and Luigi Pirandello, followed by Federico Fellini and numerous Hollywood stars, frequented it as well. The therapeutic properties of the chloride-sulphur-sodium waters that spring from the subsurface of Montecatini, together with the splendid architecture, parks and gardens, make this ancient spa centre one of the most elegant and sophisticated in Europe. Montecatini Alto, with its medieval historic centre, and Montecatini Terme (developed in the 18th century by Grand Duke Leopoldo of Lorraine) are linked by a funicular that has been active for more than one hundred years.

Four kilometres, and the asphalt strip of the motorway, separate Montecatini from Monsummano Terme, the site of the Museo d'Arte Contemporanea, celebrated for its hot springs: the Grotta Giusti, a karstic cavity that owes its name to the 19th century poet Giuseppe Giusti, and the Grotta Parlanti. Monsummano is also the biennial capital of "Cioccolosità", a three-day event that celebrates the confectionary excellence of this area of Tuscany, where one finds a high concentration of fine chocolate artisans, to the point that it has been nicknamed "Chocolate Valley".

FLOWERS AND PAPER

It is no coincidence that the hilly areas of Val di Pescia, at the border between Valdinievole and Lucchesia, are called the "Switzerland of Pescia": its landscape is dotted with ancient castles in 'pietra serena', intact villages that surround Pescia and mark out a fascinating circular itinerary for trekking enthusiasts.

Panoramic view of Montecatini Alta.

Garden of the Villa Garzoni in Collodi.

Divided in two by the river by the same name and filled with remnants of the medieval and Medici past, Pescia is the land of nursery gardening, cut flowers and house plants. Here one can find extremely rare roses, picturesque ornamental plants and camelias that boast royal clients, as well as bonsai and citrus plants.

Pescia, a city of art and culture, with its theatre named after Giovanni Pacini (a prolific opera composer who spent the last years of his life here), is historically tied to the manufacture of paper, contending with Fabriano for first place as oldest paper factory in Italy. For half a millennium it has produced this wondrous and ancient communication tool, resulting from the combination of fibre, water, wind and the labour of master paper manufacturers. In the fraction of Pietrabuona, the Museo della Carta, a point of reference on an international scale for restorers and bibliophiles, permits exploration of the paper universe and discovery of its thousand secrets, through collections of early 19th century watermarks and period machinery.

THE CITY OF PINOCCHIO

Collodi is a medieval village, just ten kilometres from Montecatini Terme, offering a cascade of houses descending down the hill as far as the splendid 17th century Villa Garzoni, connected to a Baroque-style garden with statues, water games and a "Butterfly House" hosting more than eight hundred butterflies. But Collodi is above all known as the

"city of Pinocchio", home of the puppet star of the 19th century children's story of the same name, penned by Carlo Collodi. The Florentine author, whose real name was Carlo Lorenzini, used the pseudonym 'Collodi' in homage to the birth town of his mother, where he spent his childhood. In honour of the initiation fable (a source of inspiration for art, music, theatre, comics and film), the Parco di Pinocchio, inaugurated in the mid-1950s, offers a literary journey through mosaics and sculpture, as well as a packed calendar of cultural events. From the village of Collodi, through the "Via della Fiaba", one can travel an ancient Roman road that connects the city of Pinocchio to nearby Pescia in about an hour's walk.

A WATERY PARADISE

The largest interior marshland in Italy extends south of the Pistoia Apennines, between Montalbano and the Colline delle Cerbaie: 1800 hectares divided between the provinces of Pistoia and

One rests in Pistoia as if in the arms of a noble countrywoman. There is a perfume of grass and earth mixed with that of ancient essences, of byssus from Tuscany, of noble amorous confidences. [...] Around the Piazza del Duomo one goes up and down as if in a dream. At every flight one falls into a labyrinth, but one always finds an exit flanked by arches, marble urns and camellias.

Ardengo Soffici

Left: Padule di Fucecchio, streams of water. Bottom, Illustration from Pinocchio and a mansion near Fucecchio.

Florence, soaked with flows of water from the foothills of the Apennines. The Padule di Fucecchio (Fucecchio Marshlands), a place of passage on the migratory routes of more than two hundred bird species, counts such naturalistic treasures as cranes, black storks and more than four heron species. As for flora, it also hosts "sphagnum" mosses, a trace of survival from the last ice ages, rare floating ferns, floating water lilies and carnivorous floating plants. More than 200 hectares of the Padule form a nature preserve equipped with visitor facilities, including an animal observatory. It is the perfect place for nature lovers, nature photography enthusiasts and birdwatchers, and can be visited on foot, by boat, by bicycle and on horseback.

MASSA
E CARRARA
Massa and Carrara

A detail of Piazza Aranci in Massa.

THE STONE OF ART

They're not white with snow. And yet that is undoubtedly the way they appear. Facing away from the sea and looking at the peaks of the Apuan Alps, what seem to be unending snow-white glaciers, reminiscent of the Dolomites, are actually wounds in the mountain - more than two thousand hectares of marble. That which the quarries slowly dip into and take from the rock is a miracle of geology, the purest and whitest of marbles. And the city of Carrara is the world capital. This "gleaming stone," as evoked by the Greek etymology of the word, is found in many varieties: white statuary marble ("marmo statuario"), arabesque marble ("marmo arabescato"), cipolin marble ("marmo cipollino"), and purple-violet marble ("marmo paonazzo"). These genuine treasures, already known to the ancient Romans, have always been used in art. There is no military victory that is not celebrated with marble, no royal residence that does not rely on it, nor symbol of economic or political triumph that does not require its durable lustre.

BETWEEN THE SEA AND THE MOUNTAINS

Carrara, surrounded by stony glaciers and a mountain reshaped by quarrymen, is one of Italy's oldest towns, it's beauty expressed through the presence of century-old settlements. There is no

capital in the world that does not have a remnant of Carrara, its precious marble. In addition to the museum that explains marble extraction techniques, every fountain, building or statue in the city is, down to this day, a reminder of the visceral, historical, cultural and economic connection between Carrara and the metamorphic rock of its mountains. Sung about in Dante Alighieri's *Divine Comedy*, the city offers a cosy and colourful historic centre: Piazza Alberica is covered with marble tarsia (a geometrical inlay) and surrounded by 17th and 18th century buildings. Located in the centre of the square is a marble fountain dedicated to Maria Beatrice d'Este, two hundred metres away from which lies the Duomo in Romanesque-Gothic style, which is almost entirely covered by a spectacular white marble that was quarried nearby. The rose window, composed of a hub and spokes, is similar in form to the gold wheel found on the blue background of

Carrara's coat of arms. The wheel is the emblem of a working reality which has always consisted of taking chips of stone from the giant mountain and moving them towards the sea. Situated next to the cathedral is the home of Michelangelo Buonarroti where, from 1496 until 1525, he stayed on several occasions. Just a few steps away is Palazzo Cybo Malaspina, a 16th century structure built on the ruins of a medieval castle, home to the historic Accademia di Belle Arti. Neoclassical plaster casts and models, in addition to casts by Canova, are preserved in the Academy's plaster cast collection. Located in the hamlet of Avenza, the "great tower" remains from a medieval fortress, reinforced in the 14th century by Castruccio Castracani, lord of Lucca, and in the 15th century by the Malaspina family.

PATHS THROUGH MARBLE
Winding roads and lunar landscapes lead all the way into the marble's secrets,

Above, sunset over the sea, sculptors' atelier, Piazza Alberica in Carrara.
Right: Carrara 's Cathedral and statue of Neptune.

among blocks and slabs positioned or dragged by trucks and accumulated rubble (in the so-called "ravaneti"). The old routes are perfect challenges for climbers, while the Parco Regionale delle Alpi Apuame, which flows into the province of Lucca, offers trails, refuges and faunal oases. The quarries exhibit the age-old challenge of man seeking to dominate nature. Today, the industry employs twelve thousand people and contributes significantly to the province's economy, alongside the increasing touristic marina-related activity. Colonnata, five hundred metres above sea level, was founded in Roman times as a settlement for quarry slaves. Its quarries are the most impressive of the Apuan basins, with a view that mustn't be missed of the famous quarry complexes in the surrounding ranges, including Monte Spallone. Another basin, Ravaccione, can be admired from Belvedere di Campocecina; a natural stage, 1190 metres above sea level, offering views of the impressive marble fields, the city of Carrara, its commercial port (Marina di Carrara) and the entire Versilian Riviera.

Above, pathways cut through the marble of the Apuan Alps. Left, Carrara Qarries.

WHITE GOLD OF FANTISCRITTI

A trip to the quarries of Fantiscritti involves the pleasant discovery of the now decommissioned marble railway, built in the last quarter of the nineteenth century to connect the basins' storage centres with the sawmills on the plain and with the port. The transport of marble by rail stopped in the 1960s but the Ponti di Vara (Bridges of Vara) still stand and were later used for the transit of trucks. The name "Fantiscritti" comes from the aedicule carved into a wall of the quarry eighteen centuries ago: the bas-relief, now in the Accademia di Carrara, features figures that were first interpreted as children - "soldiers" in

fact - besides which are "signatures" or writings ("scritti") carved by many visitors, including Canova. Unlike the open air, stepped quarries that whiten the Apuan Alps, Fantiscritti is an internal quarry; its tunnel entrance taps into the vein of marble located in the bowels of the mountain. This underground cathedral consists of huge environments marked by pillars, ten to fifteen metres wide, and a constant temperature of 16 °C. Here, blocks up to ten metres high are cut to be turned into obelisks and statues. Everywhere, there are reflections of light and puddles, calling to mind the importance of the water used to cool the cutting equipment.

GASTRONOMIC REPOSITORIES

Not only marble; food for art and architecture. Northern Tuscany boasts an original culinary tradition of distinct and fascinating products. Taking a closer look, though, it becomes clear that marble plays a role also in the production of the renowned Lardo di Colonnata, from one of the previously mentioned villages of the Apuan Alps. The lard is rubbed and seasoned with garlic in marble basins, alternating layers of pork mixed with pepper, cinnamon, clove, coriander, sage and rosemary. This "noble" food, which provided energy to quarry workers, resembles the "white gold" of these areas - white in colour and veined with shades of pink. Another speciality of Lunigiana, between Tuscany and Liguria, are testaroli. This dish, like the land where it comes from, has thousands of years of history and simple, authentic ingredients consisting of only flour, water and salt. The term comes from the "testo," i.e. the container - at one time in clay, today in cast iron - on which the smooth batter is cooked over a wood fire. The resulting discs are then cut into diamond shapes and placed in boiling water for a few minutes (with the flame completely out), covered with chestnut leaves and drained. Finally they are dressed, as their highly porous nature makes for easy absorption of various sauces such as olive oil with pecorino cheese or tomato sauce with porcini mushrooms. However, a tasty rule is to couple them with the intense green of basil, using a world renowned condiment - pesto.

Top, Ponti di Vara, Fantiscritti Quarries. Above and left, Testaroli and Lard of Colonnata.

MASSA, AT THE FOOT OF THE APUAN ALPS

Massa's Duomo is just seven kilometres from the Duomo of Carrara. Situated on the soft rolling hills at the foot of the Apuan Alps, Massa establishes its beauty through Roman, Medieval and Renaissance remains. The Castello Malaspina, formed by a large complex that includes "la Rocca" (the fortress), overlooks the city. The castle dates back to the twelfth century; the architectural complex, transformed into a prison in the nineteenth century, is now open to the public and is divided into three units: the walls with ramparts and trenches, the residence and the keep. The city is divided into two parts: the upper medieval portion, and the lower portion centred around Piazza Aranci, home of the Palazzo Ducale (Doge's Palace; formerly called Palazzo Cybo Malaspina, after the family that ruled the city and increased development in the sixteenth and seventeenth centuries). Three kilometres further on, following the scent of the sea, the Museo Etnologico delle Apuane offers one of Tuscany's most comprehensive collections of work tools and industrial and agricultural equipment related to the productive activities and daily life of the local people over the past two centuries. And just a few steps away, there's the sea; the coast of Carrara and Massa, with its sandy beaches and numerous outfitted camp sites.

ALPS OF TUSCANY

He was a young injured fugitive from Pisa; she was the daughter of the shepherd from Garfagnana who took him into his hut and tended to him. Enamoured, she tried in vain to learn his name and eventually called him Pisanino. At the young man's death, the young shepherdess cried everyday and her tears turned to stone, creating the tallest mountain in the meadow. Down to this day, quarrymen find shimmers of those of just over 2000 metres, while the summit of Monte Sagro (1749 metres) offers breathtaking views of Carrara and the Tyrrhenian Sea. The morphologically rugged and spectacular Apuan Alps are full of wildlife. They are livened up by caves

Lunigiana.

tears of mourning in the quartz crystals, a poetic trace of that sad love. This is one of the many legends that have blossomed in the Apuan Alps. Monte Pisanino is the range's highest peak and lies between the provinces of Massa Carrara and Lucca at an elevation and the "Vie di Lizza", ancient trails dug along the mountain sides, used to transport the blocks of marble downhill.

LUNIGIANA

The far north of Tuscany is a magical territory that exudes history and that has not given in to tourist compromises. The ancient road known as the "Via Francigena" passed through this secluded area, and was part of the route travelled by thousands of religious pilgrims heading to Rome and other holy places, as well as by armies, merchants and artists. It

Lunigiana, in the upper and middle valley of the River Magra, there are innumerable castles and fortified villages, among these: the town of Fivizzano in the Parco Nazionale dell'Appennino Tosco-Emiliano, with its walls erected by order of Cosimo de' Medici in 1540, and the Castello

is a stretch of land, spread among woods of beech and chestnut, that nuzzles into Emilia and stubbornly guards its traditions (including culinary ones).

The historical region takes its name from Luni, once a prosperous Roman colony, now in the province of La Spezia. In

della Verrucola, a spectacular example of medieval architecture.

Fivizzano is also home to the Museo della Stampa Jacopo da Fivizzano (a printing museum): this small town pioneered moveable typefaces and began printing books in 1470–71,

> *From the Palace of Versailles in France to the Roman Pantheon, from the statues of Michelangelo to those of Canova, from the Pietà to Cupid and Psyche, it is from this part of Tuscany that the raw material is taken from nature and transformed into art.*
> *Andrea Bocelli*

eleven years before Vienna, nine years before London and seven years before Geneva and Barcelona. Treasures of ancient urban development are found in medieval Pontremoli, the principle town of the Lunigiana, featuring the Castello di Piagnaro that protects it from on high and a literary award that amplifies its name on an international level.
Moving towards Villafranca reveals ancient mills and an important Ethnographic Museum. Continuing all the way down to the valley floor, the family of Napoleon is said to have originated here, in Stadano Bonaparte. On towards Caprigliola, getting much closer to Liguria, the slender cylindrical sandstone watchtower renders the land's profile similar to that of a fascinating and bizzare ship, drying on the side of the River Magra. Mulazzo deserves to be treated separately, and not just because Dante was hosted here in 1306 by Fransceschino Malaspina. With its stone houses, narrow streets, and interesting monuments, such as the church devoted to St. Nicholas and the Torre di Dante (Tower of Dante), Mulazzo is one of the Lunigiana's most evocative towns. Nearby, a thirteenth century building houses the Museo Dantesco Lunigianese.

Above, Pradilinara Lunigiana.
Left, stele statues.

STELE STATUES

Men with daggers; women with stylised features; stone faces looking at us from afar, from a distance of just over five thousand years. These are the stele statues found in Lunigiana - anthropomorphic menhirs in hard sandstone. Dating from between the late prehistoric age and the arrival of the Romans, these monuments of obscure symbolic significance could possibly be divinities, heroes or even funerary monuments. The oldest stele statues have no mouth - metaphor of a soul still preserved inside the stone. In the early 1900's, nine such statues were found on tilling the land in Ponte Vecchio, near Fivizzano. They were ordered in a row according to height, with their faces pointed towards the arc of the sun. One of the most recent findings was in 2005 in the Commune of Mulazzo. The originals or plaster copies of almost all those found to date are collected in the Museo delle Statue Stele at the previously mentioned Castello di Pagnaro in Pontremoli.

And I remember the summers with Montale, in Forte dei Marmi. Every day we would meet up with the likes of Henry Moore, Marino Marini, Guttuso. Montale was always drawing: the sea, the Apuan Alps...

Carla Fracci

ONE HUNDRED CHURCHES

Five hundred years of freedom add their weight to the history of this place. Lucca was an independent republic until the beginning of the nineteenth century, but continued to cultivate its own peculiarities as a tolerant, creative centre of enlightenment. The perpendicular streets and portions of the walls are remnants of the ancient Roman urban infrastructure. The perfectly intact walls date the historic centre back to the Renaissance era and are a symbol of the city. These walls, which extend over more than four kilometres and feature eleven ramparts, have seen no war damage. In the 1800s the wall area was converted into an urban park punctuated by meadows and shaded by plane trees, red oaks and chestnut trees: an ideal leisure setting and stage for Lucca's main events. Rising from the wall of the city of a hundred churches are the Torre delle Ore and the 14th century Torre Guinigi, of stone and brick, fringed – almost as if the set of a fairy tale – by a few holm oaks on its summit. The entire city, perfect to explore on foot, is full of places of worship and elegant

LUCCA

Lucca, aerial view.

Above, Piazza dell'Anfiteatro in Lucca. Top right, along the city streets.

buildings. Such is the case along via Fillungo, the lively business and commercial centre, full of medieval elements.

The elegance of Lucca's architectural civilization is refracted in the countryside surrounding the city, dotted with villas from the Renaissance and Baroque eras: true works of art conceived as summer residences of the wealthy Lucchese.

ARCHITECTURAL WONDERS

Built on the ruins of the Roman amphitheatre, perfect in its closed elliptical form, is one of the most unique piazzas in Italy. With its fifty-five arches, Piazza dell'Anfiteatro - or Piazza del Mercato - is set in the ancient heart of the city, and has been gradually filled with buildings since the Middle Ages. It was only in 1830 that Lucchese architect Lorenzo Nottolini restored the ancient structure, freeing up interior space and building the path that follows the profile of the square on the outside. Nottolini is also responsible for the Roman-style aqueduct, which was completed in the mid-nineteenth century: more than three kilometres

long with 460 brick and stone arches, the aqueduct ends outside the walls of Lucca, in the Tempietto di San Concordio, a small circular neoclassical Doric temple with two large marble basins and pipes supplying fountains and fountain heads. The aqueduct, split into two to allow access to the A11 motorway, now functions as a monument rather than to supply water.

PUCCINI ITINERARIES IN LUCCA

Giacomo Puccini (1858-1924), the composer of *Manon Lescaut*, *La Bohème*, *Madame Butterfly*, *Tosca* and *Turandot*, came from a long line of Lucca born musicians. He was born in the historic city centre, at n.9, Corte San Lorenzo. He was baptised in the Chiesa dei Santi Giovanni e Reparata, and made his debut as a composer, at nineteen years of age, in the church devoted to the saints Paolino and Donato. As a boy, he played the organ in the Cathedral of San Martino, while in 1878 - when he was still studying music at the "Pacini" institute, later called "Boccherini" - he performed at the Teatro del Giglio as an accompanying pianist. Today, the same

Above, a monument to Giacomo Puccini. Left, Torre Guinigi.

theatre houses a bas-relief of the Maestro himself. A famous café in via Fillungo bears a plaque commemorating Puccini as one of the locale's greatest patrons. He is depicted in various statues in the city and at the house where he was born, which was restored and converted into a museum, displaying the original furnishings of his formative years, as well as music, documents, paintings and various memorabilia.

NOT ONLY OPERA

Being the birthplace of Puccini and of his almost–contemporary Alfredo Catalani (1854-1893), author of *La Wally* and *Loreley*, would be enough to indicate Lucca as a Mecca of music. But Lucca also boasts important names in the field of instrument production, such as Francesco Geminiani (1687-1762) and, above all, Luigi Boccherini (1743–1805), a prolific composer and excellent cellist, and founder - along with Giuseppe Tartini, Pietro Nardini, and fellow countryman Filippo Manfredi - of the first professional string quartet. A pioneer of 18th century music history, Charles Burney, defines his works as "excellent compositions, better than those of any other musician of our time, excepting Haydn." Lucca has honoured his memory with a study centre and a plaque in via Fillungo, where he was born.

CULINARY CULTURE

Even the gastronomic specialities, no less than the museums, tell the story of a city and the depth of its civilization. In Lucca, spelt - perhaps the oldest kind of grain - dominates soups, enriched with

*Above: Ponte della
Maddalena over
the River Serchio.
Right, Barga and
Castelvecchio Pascoli.*

pinto beans and of course with olive oil and aromas from the surrounding hills. Garmugia soup is a variant offered in spring: a refined balance of contrasting flavours, from artichokes to broad beans, enriched with croutons. Among other specialties are the porridge made from pinto beans and black cabbage, the fresh pasta "tordelli" and the baked vegetables pies. As for desserts, offering is particularly varied: from "Buccellato," (a very fragrant cake with anise seeds), to Zuppa Lucchese (Buccellato softened in vin santo and filled with strawberries flavoured in wine and cream), "torte dei bischeri" (a type of chocolate cake), and "necci": crêpes of chestnut flour served with fresh ricotta.

THE RIVER PARK

A large park was built between Lucca and the River Serchio that flows through the province: an area of 250 hectares that surrounds the banks and is divided into three different routes - a nature trail, a route through the water itself and a historical trail - for walking, hiking, cycling, mountain biking, horseback riding, kayaking or canoeing. This gathering place immersed in the countryside contains soccer fields, space for archery and skateboarding, as well as a bowling alley and areas for operating model cars and model aeroplanes. At the entrance of the park, the panoramic Terrazza Petroni pays homage to the famous Lucchese writer, and is a preferred place to stop, decorated in harmony with nature, from the cobblestone pathways to the trees.

BARGA

History and beauty, steep narrow streets, craft shops, medieval monuments, Renaissance buildings: this is Barga, the most important centre of the Media Valle del Serchio, which, surrounded by walls, rises four hundred feet high, dominating the Garfagnana. At the fulcrum of the historic city centre is the Duomo, whose original construction dates back to the year one thousand. To its left is the Palazzo Pretorio (Praetorian Palace; built in the thirteenth century), which houses the Museo Civico del Territorio, displaying Paleolithic fossils, ancient artefacts and burial items. Between the Duomo and the Palazzo del Podestà is the Arringo, a vast meadow where the people gathered, and an exceptional vantage point that embraces the Alps and the Apennines. Tolls from the Duomo's bell tower inspired the famous poem *L'ora di Barga,* by Giovanni Pascoli, who for a long time lived in the hamlet now called Castelvecchio Pascoli. His 18th century villa is a museum and the adjacent chapel houses his tomb.

UPPER GARFAGNANA

In the Lucchese Appenine range, the Riserva Naturale Lamarossa covers a forest of nearly 170 hectares of chestnut, Turkey oak and white fir trees. A peat bog, surrounded by a beech wood, is crossed by numerous streams. A wetland of great natural interest, with rare flora, can be visited along marked routes, starting from the Centro Visitatori dell'Orecchiella. Nearby, don't miss out on Castelnuovo Garfagnana, a place onece governed by the poet Ludovico

Ariosto, between 1522 and 1525. Its fortress Rocca Ariostesca, renovated several times between the Middle Ages and the Renaissance, houses the Museo Archeologico. Every Thursday an extensive market of "stalls," which dates back to medieval times, fills the streets and squares of the historic centre: an occasion so significant that the old laws prohibited arrests from being made on Thursdays so as not to disturb the market. Castelnuovo provides access to the main tourist destinations of the Valle del Serchio, such as trekking, walking, cycling and equestrian trails.

SPAS CENTRES, SPORTS AND NATURE

"A genuine paradise in the wild" is how the German Romantic poet Heinrich Heine describes the Bagni, or Baths, of Lucca, one of the Italy's largest mountain towns, with its twenty-five scattered hamlets. This spa locality was already popular in the Middle Ages, thanks to the healing properties of the bicarbonate and calcium sulphate in its spring waters. Among its distinguished guests were Dante and Boccaccio (who set one of his stories here), poets such as George Byron, Carducci and Eugenio Montale, and musicians of the calibre of Gioachino Rossini, Giuseppe Verdi, Pietro Mascagni and Giacomo Puccini. Nearby, in the Riserva Naturale dell'Orrido Botri, a limestone gorge along the Rio Pelago offers a view of one of the deepest canyons in Italy (which is said to have inspired the first Cantica of Dante's *Inferno*, from his *Divine Comedy*). This district is a preferred nesting site for the golden eagle and is now a nature reserve,

open to visitors (entry from Ponte a Gaio) between June and September.
At these latitudes, those who practice sports have an overwhelming choice: rafting or canoeing, mountain biking or horseback riding (with 250 km of "Garfagnana Turismo Equestre" trails), hiking along historical paths, or the many caves that are a spelunker's joy.

THE LAKE SANCTUARY OF OPERA

Torre del Lago Puccini, a hamlet of Viareggio, is a small town between Lake Massaciuccoli and the Tyrrhenian Sea, and is the place where the composer from Lucca lived for nearly a quarter of a century, where he composed - on his Forster piano - works such as *Madame Butterfly*, *La fanciulla del West*, *La Rondine* and *Il Trittico*. Appreciated for its coastline and its ferrous sand that gives life to the green glass of Empoli (a town renowned for its glass-makers), it has large historic buildings such as Villa Borbone, the 19th century residence of the Duchess of Lucca and currently home to exhibitions and shows. At the beginning of the last decade of the 19th century, Giacomo Puccini moved to Torre del Lago. With the proceeds of his first successes, in 1899 he built a villa overlooking the water, personally taking care of its Art Nouveau interior. Here he spent his time between composing, hunting and nights of partying with friends (as is summed up in the Maestro's definition of himself: "A mighty hunter of wild birds, opera librettos and beautiful women"). The villa now houses the Museo Villa Puccini. Visitors can still find his shotguns, many manuscripts, and his

Torre del Lago Puccini.

piano. His tomb is in the villa's chapel. In 1938, Puccini's name was added to the original name "Torre del Lago." At the summer festival, named after the genius from Lucca, Puccini's operas are performed in a spectacular, impressive open-air theatre, built on the lake shore.

VERSILIA

An immense beach of fine sand; a tangible legend of beauty, history and high society; a landscape that evokes holiday and the pleasures of life among the green sea, the smell of pines and the mountainous background of the Apuan Alps; between the tennis courts and golf courses and the sweet aura of the good life, which here has never ended. The Grandeur was inaugurated in the early decades of the 19th century, with the decision of Maria Luisa of Bourbon (Infanta of Spain, Duchess of Lucca) to build the first wet dock in Viareggio and with the construction, commissioned by Pauline Bonaparte (and her companion at the time, the composer Giovanni Pacini), of a villa in Viareggio, in 1822. The so-called "Refuge of Venus", the last home of Napoleon's sister, was erected in the exact spot where the sea returned the body of the poet Percy Bysshe Shelley, who died at the age of thirty in a shipwreck; today it is a museum and hosts a gallery dedicated to contemporary art. At the beginning of the twentieth century, Versilia established itself as a preferred destination for elite tourists, whole filled the Liberty villas of the pine groves, as

Above, beach in Versilia. Right, Carnival of Viareggio.

well as the hotels, dance halls and locales of a small town turned Art-Déco. A prime example is the Gran Caffè Margherita, where it was possible to meet the likes of Guglielmo Marconi and Giacomo Puccini. Nowadays, the Versilia coast maintains its supremacy as the most glamorous in the region, thanks to the many night-life establishments overlooking the sea.

VIAREGGIO IN CARNIVAL

The Carnival of Viareggio is spectacular, grotesque, ironic and often sarcastic - an event that peacefully turns Lucca's outlet to the sea...upside down. The traditional parade of allegorical floats was founded in 1873 when some of the middle-class, at the tables of a café in Viareggio's Via Regia, decided to dress up in protest against taxes. Soon they began building triumphal wagons, monuments built by local carpenters from the shipyards. With the introduction of light-weight paper-pulp in the 1920s, it became possible to create colossal allegorical floats; starting in the 1950s early Italian TV captured and enhanced much of this merry irony. The historic symbol of the Carnival of Viareggio is the mask of Burlamacco: a clownish character designed in a futuristic style, highlighting the predilections of it's creator, Umberto Bonetti, a graphic designer from Viareggio.

FORTE DEI MARMI

It's on the waterfront of Forte dei Marmi that we thought we would end this collection of evocations, this meagre handful of clues from which to start exploring one's very own Tuscany. Because, let us remember, this is a region

of the soul (and indeed, perhaps without even knowing it, this is what we have always thought). It is a land we carry in our hearts; the adopted homeland of anyone who elevates it to such. Forte dei Marmi is a metaphor for life's compelling beauty. Exclusive yet welcoming, the soft salt water of its seas run right through it, in the gardens and tree-lined avenues, in the shade of its many pine groves and its scattered holm oaks. Its "little fort", the 18th century coastal stronghold called "Lorrenese", now the Museo della Satira

e della Caricatura (Museum of Satire and Caricature), is not at all threatening but rather expresses the placid solidity of a destination that is joyful and spiritual, a place of sweet winter melancholy and sheer summer elation.

The old jetty is an outstretched arm that for many centuries has been lending its hand to the Mediterranean. It extends for over three hundred metres offering, to those who walk it, the best sunsets, and the most exciting postcard views of the "marble" coast. The list of cultural, political, industrial and artistic personalities who

preferred Forte dei Marmi and frequented its historic places, is mind-boggling: intellectuals such as Eugenio Montale, Giuseppe Ungaretti and Primo Levi; singers such as Edith Piaf , Mina and Ray Charles; industrialists such as Agnelli, Barilla, Marzotto... And of course, the world's best loved "Voice of Tuscany," Andrea Bocelli, who for many years has chosen to live here. It can happen that, walking along one of the avenues close to the sea, one can distinguish the unmistakable timbre of his voice from over the wall of his dwelling overlooking the beach. His voice is as sincere and as deep as his beloved region; a song that Tuscany carries within its very soul, embodying, as we have said, the culture of its land made of intense relationships, generosity, common sense, healthy food, beauty, and the art of 'doing' with love.

Space for your own "**Voice of Tuscany**":

....

....

....

Left, beach in Versilia. Top, a smile,
and a final farewell from Andrea.

Bibliography

Andrea Bocelli, *The Music of Silence*, Istituto Geografico De Agostini, Novara 2010
Andrea Bocelli, *Tuscan Skies*, DVD Sugar, Milan 2001
Arte e Storia della Toscana, Bonechi, Florence 2006
Feste e tradizioni popolari della Toscana, Newton Compton, Rome 2006
Grand Tour Toscana, Istituto Geografico De Agostini, Novara 2004
Guida turistica e cartografica delle province d'Italia, Automobile Club d'Italia
Italia. Volume 2 Toscana, Istituto Geografico De Agostini, Novara 2009

Niccolò Rinaldi, *Secret Florence*, Jonglez, Versailles 2011
Onde. Percorsi nel paesaggio letterario della Toscana, Edizioni Polistampa, Florence 2001
Tesori d'Italia. Toscana, Euroed, Milan 2004
Toscana Clup Guide, Istituto Geografico De Agostini, Novara 2006
Toscana e Umbria, EDT, Turin 2010
Toscana. Le autentiche ricette della tradizione. I prodotti tipici e i vini, Boroli, Milan 2007
Toscana Turismo dalla A alla Z, Istituto Geografico De Agostini, Novara 2009
Toscana. Tutti i colori del viaggio, GuideGo, Istituto Geografico De Agostini, Novara 2006-2007

Quotations

Ardengo Soffici, *La giostra dei sensi*. Florence, Vallecchi, Florence 1918
Carla Fracci, *Lo spettacolo della mia vita*, Leonardo Arte, 1996
Charles Dickens, *Pictures from Italy*, London 1846
Curzio Malaparte, *Salutami Livorno* in the volume *Il dorato sole dell'inferno etrusco*,
    Franco Cesati Editore, Florence 1985
Eugenio Montale, from an interview with Eugenio Montale conducted by Sandro Briosi
    on *Uomini e idee*, March-April 1966, now in *Immagini di una vita* by F. Contorbia, Mondadori 1985

Giosuè Carducci, *Rime Nuove*, Libro II – XXXIV, 1906
Henry James, *Ore italiane. Città toscane*, 1874
Michelangelo Buonarroti, *Rime*, Garzanti Editore 2006
Pëtr Il'i Čajkovskij, *Ciajkovskij a Firenze. Storia di un'anima* by Leonardo Previero,
    edited by Luca Giannelli, Scramasax, Florence 2006
William Dean Howells, *Tuscan Cities*, New York 1867

REGIONE TOSCANA
Culture, Tourism and Trade Council
www.regione.toscana.it

TOSCANA PROMOZIONE
Economic Promotion Agency
of Tuscany
Villa Fabbricotti
Via Vittorio Emanuele II, 62-64
Florence
www.toscanapromozione.it

For more information on destinations
in Tuscany:
www.turismo.intoscana.it

Regione Toscana

TOSCANA
PROMOZIONE

POR
CReO
2007-13

UNIONE EUROPEA
FONDO EUROPEO
DI SVILUPPO REGIONALE